Black Angel

I'm Bipolar too. This is _my_ story.

Written by Ryan McCoy

Edited by Lisa McCoy

This book is dedicated in loving memory of my Black Angel, Dutch.

CHAPTER ONE: FIGHTING DEMONS..4

CHAPTER TWO: GOING TO CALIFORNIA............................17

CHAPTER THREE: HOLLYWOOD UNDEAD...........................27

CHAPTER FOUR: A HOME IN TOPANGA...........................35

CHAPTER FIVE: TIME...43

CHAPTER SIX: LIFE & DEATH.....................................53

CHAPTER SEVEN: REMEMBRANCE...............................67

CHAPTER EIGHT: TUESDAY, MARCH 28, 2017.......................75

CHAPTER NINE: THE TOP OF A MOUNTAIN.......................89

AFTERWORD...97

CHAPTER ONE: FIGHTING DEMONS

I was maybe 23 or 24 years old. I was working as a car salesman at Dwayne Lane's Chrysler/Jeep in Everett, Washington, my home town. I was living in the same house I had grown up in, but no longer with my mom; I was now living with my dad. I had asked him a few times about getting a dog. I remember him not saying no, but not really saying yes either. I enjoyed that, because I felt like I was maturing and this would be more of an adult decision. This would be *my* dog. I already knew what I was going to name him before I got to the shelter.

I had been noodling around the idea for a couple of weeks and finally, one day after work, I went to the shelter by my home to go look at dogs. I was wearing my "nice clothes" at the time, which consisted of my brother's hand-me-down slacks, shirt, and oversized tie. I thought I looked fly as hell, though.

I had been to the shelter the day before to kind of check it out and see how much it would cost. I remember walking down the rows of concrete, staring at the various dogs caged up. I didn't really have a specific breed in mind—I just wanted a dog-looking dog. You know? Not one with a smashed face, not a tiny one, not a huge one, one that I felt fit me.

You see, we always had dogs growing up. There was Sunny, who was my mom's and had since passed. Scruffy, who was my sister's, had also passed, and then there was Caesar. A gift originally meant for my brother, but he got too busy with high school life that he bonded with the person who took care of him most often. That person happened to be my mom. But this dog would be mine. I didn't want it to look like the other dogs we had.

I remember feeling slightly disappointed that I wouldn't be getting my dog that day. I had looked in most of the cages, but I didn't see anything I liked. Except one. He was young, 9 to 10 months or so. He was all black with a white diamond shape on his throat. He stood up as I walked past his cage and wiggled his tail. I bent down and put my hand in for him to lick. I was so excited because this dog looked perfect. I couldn't believe no one had taken him yet.

The woman at the shelter asked if I'd like to go out back with him and play a bit to see if we got along. I remember thinking to myself, no, it's cool. I'll just take him. But I didn't want them to think I was just going in blindly getting a dog. So, I said yes, and she led me to a small fenced-in area out back where I could watch him run around a bit and play with some toys. She said to take my time and left me alone with him. Not much to my surprise, I got along with him instantly. He acted and looked like a dog's dog. I couldn't be happier.

I threw the ball for him, and he ran happily to go and bring it back. I leaned down and rubbed his face and asked, "Are you Dutch? Huh? Are you Dutch? You want to come home with me?" Then, in typical Dutch fashion, he leapt up with his front paws and ripped a huge hole in my pant legs, and I said, "You mother fucker..." I took it as a sign and purchased my dog and named him Dutch.

I filled out the proper paperwork and paid the $60 or so. The lady informed me that all dogs bought from a shelter who aren't neutered need to be. There was a vet they used, and I could pick up Dutch the next day from there. They let me say goodbye to Dutch, and I remember getting a strange feeling when I bent down and looked him in the eyes to tell him I would see him tomorrow. We had only known each other for maybe a total of 30 minutes, but there was sadness in his eyes to see me go. I thought, dude, chill. We just met; I'll see you in a day. I didn't instantly fall in love with Dutch, but I'm pretty sure that he did with me.

I went home excited and told my dad all about how he had ripped my pants and that when he did that, I knew I had to buy him. My dad seemed genuinely excited for me as well. The next day I went to go and pick him up. He was sedated and had one of those stupid cones around his neck, and we all made fun of him for it. I brought him home and introduced him to my dad. I remember my dad's first thoughts being, wow! This dog is so calm! He didn't realize that Dutch was still medicated, and it wasn't long before he began to perk up and want to play.

We played that day, and I walked him and was excited about the new responsibility and experience. I remember thinking, I'm going to raise the coolest dog in the world. He's gonna be the type of dog that I don't even need to put a leash on, because he and I will be *that* close. He'll be my "Mad Max" dog.

That night, we crawled into bed to watch a movie. The one thing I discovered about Dutch that night is that he made for a *great* cuddler. Unlike popular belief, I fucking LOVE to cuddle. I turned all the lights off and put on my favorite movie ever made, *Predator*. I am a child of the '80s. Arnold Schwarzenegger was, and still is, my favorite actor of all time. My dad wasn't around much when I was growing up, and then my parents split, so I was always finding men to look up to. Arnold is one of those men. Not only is his physical presence near god-like, but his personal story always inspired me. It still does. Not only did a kid in Austria come from nothing, but his dreams were out of this world. Everyone told him he couldn't do it, but he never listened to them and followed his dreams anyway, and he won. He achieved them ALL. I have always known I want to be the biggest filmmaker to have ever lived, and so I aspire to be able to achieve the same level of success as he has. I've been making movies since I was in fifth grade, and was acting and re-creating scenes from movies with my friends since before then. Movies are my life. Period. And they will continue to be everything for me until the day I die. I already know it in my head—there's no doubt in my mind that I will build something BIG and IMPACTFUL for everyone in the world to become a part of.

In the film, Arnie's character's name is "Dutch," hence why I had the name picked out before I ever even thought of getting a dog. I curled up with Dutch, spooning style, so his face could see the screen. That moment during the opening credits where Arnold jumps out on the helicopter after just lighting his cigar, and the camera is low-angle, and Alan Silvestri's beautiful score is drumming in the background, I whispered into Dutch's ear, "That's who you're named after...Dutch. That's your name," and then proceeded to watch the rest of the movie and fell asleep.

I had no idea at the time—how could I?—but this dog would not only save me from myself, but eventually lead me to a place I know I was meant to be at to experience an event and receive a message from whatever it is that created everything in the known universe. The majority of human beings worship and pray to a version of this, whether it be God, Allah, Buddha, whatever. I don't give it a name anymore because I know it doesn't matter. I have seen the other side, and I know why I was put on this planet and what I am meant to do. That is why I consider Dutch to be my angel. The reason I titled this book *My Black Angel* is that the road to receiving that message the night of March 28, 2017, was and is still filled with some really dark shit.

* * *

Dutch would literally do anything for food. This book is going to be FILLED with stories of not only what Dutch ate but also how much, and how he got it. Dutch's story was that he was found in the flatlands area between Everett and a neighboring city, Lake Stevens. They're not sure how long he lived there or how he lived and what he ate. I'm pretty sure Dutch never lost that scavenger mentality. Any opportunity for him to eat food, whether it were alive or dead, never went away.

I thought I would teach him cool tricks, like pretend to fall down dead after I shot him with my finger pistols. Or I could train him to go upstairs and get me a beer out of the refrigerator. Stupid stuff like that. He actually got pretty good at the gun one, but I don't think anybody ever really saw him do it, so they didn't believe me. My dad grew to like him as well. Dutch was always just so chill. When he wanted something, he'd walk up and sit and stare at you and then give this really annoying bark letting you know he wanted something, but other than that, he just kind of laid around. It was nice.

I'll continue to talk about the scary-ass path I was headed down, but first I'd like to tell you about how I was able to make my first feature-length film.

I was going into the final quarter before graduation at the Art Institute of Seattle. The dean of the video production department called me into his office one day. He and I had a really good relationship, as he also had written some screenplays, and the two of us even shared scripts with one another. I came into his office and sat down, and he said that he had made a mistake. You see, the quarter before I had met with him and gone over my credits and classes to make sure that I had enough/would have enough credits completed in my last quarter in order to graduate at the same time as all of my friends. All seemed good. Well, when he told me that day he had made a mistake, he had made a mistake all right.

I wasn't going to have enough credits to get my diploma. I asked how this could have happened. We went through it together last quarter. He gave his most sincere apologies and told me I would still be able to walk across stage and "graduate" with my friends but that I would have to come back and take one more class to fulfill the credits requirement. I was pretty pissed. He told me if there was anything he could do to help facilitate that, he would. I had already been planning on making a feature film, so here's what I told him. I would come back and take my final class, but I was going to take one quarter off. I told him that during that time off, I wanted exclusive rights to any and all production gear I wanted, whenever I wanted. He agreed and wrote a letter and gave it to the gear rental people (we called it The Cage, I believe). They were not happy with it, and neither were other students. I would walk straight to the front of the line and hand them my equipment list and they were forced to oblige. I'd take every fucking light, every camera, every C-stand, every gel, every sandbag, fucking anything I wanted. And that's how we were able to make *black* the next quarter. I still think that's a gangster-ass move and can't believe I did it.

I upheld my end of the bargain and came back the quarter after and took my final class. It was a music video production class, which I genuinely enjoyed. So why do I still not have a diploma from there? I decided not to make my final payment for tuition. I had completed everything I needed to and didn't give a shit about having a piece of paper that says I did. Later on, I would do the same thing at UCLA and not finish by one class. I had already learned everything I needed to.

So, by now I was working on the edit for my film *black*. The director, Claude, and I would sit for hours upon hours at my computer editing. Long nights, little sleep. You see, there was a deeper reason why I wanted to get Dutch that very few people knew about or believed. Looking back, I still can't say that something otherworldly was going on, but I'm also well aware that I was probably going through a manic period of my life. Oh, I've also been diagnosed with bipolar disorder. Let me try and explain.

The house I grew up in has always had a feeling to it. I experienced many things as a child that I can say with 100% certainty, definitely DID happen that I could never explain.

The figure outside my bedroom window, the elevator on my Fisher-Price garage set moving up and down on its own at night, and just the overall mood of the place. Never evil or negative, but I was always aware of SOMETHING. With everything that's happened to me over the past year, it's interesting to look back and try and discern reality from fantasy, knowing now that I've been bipolar all of my life, but I always thought I was so normal. Try and wrap your head around that for a second, because I'm still trying to do the same. Was I manic when I was five or six years old and a black figure came to my window? Was that my disease? I grew up sure that it was a bigfoot. My mother, God bless her, never doubted me for a second. I don't believe in bigfoot anymore. I believe that was my Black Angel. You see, I wasn't afraid. Never afraid. Fear came later. Fear was what I experienced during those few months before I got Dutch.

We were doing some pretty fucked-up shit for *black*. I set a jar of worms on fire, I burned a wooden cross, I was desecrating a Catholic church just to get a cool close-up of Jesus hanging on the cross above the alter just to use as an insert. I felt a darkness growing inside of me. I FELT it. My behavior was changing. I was somehow subconsciously creating a negative aura, and it was centering in on the house, specifically the room I was staying in. I was seeing shadows everywhere and having some of most vivid nightmares you can possibly imagine. I was also not sleeping, wasn't diagnosed, was drinking and pill popping way too much, and was constantly working. That film itself began to build a negative energy about it.

One night, I woke up at about 5:00 AM. I had a vision in my mind of my father dying. I was so scared, because it was so real to me. Something in me told me I had to go upstairs and see if he was alive. I told myself that was ridiculous. I fought back and forth with it for about 20 minutes before finally getting out of bed and heading upstairs. I stopped at the end of the hallway, trying to talk myself out of going and knocking on his door. I think I may have even walked back downstairs, only to turn around and come back up. The house was dead quiet and no lights were on whatsoever. I probably stood outside his bedroom door for five minutes before knocking as lightly as I could. My heart was pounding.

I quietly creaked the door open. "Dad?" I said in a tone above a whisper. "Dad?" I heard nothing. No movement. In my head I'm thinking what does this mean? You just had a vision that your father died and now you're right? Suddenly, I heard movement. Shifting of the sheets. My eyes adjusted to the dark, and I could see my dad sit up and his girlfriend move to the side. "Ryan? What's going on?" I immediately sputtered something saying sorry, I had a nightmare and I had to come and make sure you're alive, sorry, go back to bed, and I backed out of the room and closed the door.

I went back downstairs torn between the reality of what I had heard and felt and the embarrassment of waking my dad up at five in the morning. The feeling I had was so real, so true. I didn't go back to sleep. Instead, I watched a movie. Movies were always my escape. They just never let me down. Not like I think every movie is good—I just mean movies never let me down. Whether it was going through the death of my grandfather or the separation and divorce of my parents, movies were always there for me. To escape. Looking back now, I know why. It's not an easy place, my brain. I think it would scare most of you what goes on in there, especially before I was medicated or even had the slightest thought that my brain worked differently. I knew I had a high IQ, but I thought that was it. I thought all people with a genius-level IQ had brains that worked like mine. Boy, was I wrong. I've met some pretty normal geniuses in my day. But movies never disappointed me. Good or bad, they were always a way for me to shut my mind off. They were the only medication I had, even though I didn't consciously realize it.

Now, I can't blame my dad for not recognizing something was really wrong, or at least talking about it with me the next day—we all do the best we can, I get it—but this is one example of the reason I'm writing this book and telling my story: so the same pitfalls and traps I fell into mentally can be seen as signs and bring awareness to mental health disorders, and maybe we can help save a life or two. Whaddya say?

* * *

The visions and unexplainable happenings were getting more frequent and more violent. I remember one day my best friend, who remains to this day a very important person in my life, stopped by to check on me. A true friend, he knew I was going through something and wanted to make sure I was okay. He walked into my downstairs room, and I was just finishing hanging my latest drawing. I had taken a box of crayons and a pad of paper and I started drawing these visions I was having and the demons I was seeing in my nightmares. I was frantically scribbling these images down on paper, believing that somehow if I put the images out of my brain and put them on paper, they would lose their power. Shane walked in, and there were maybe 30 to 40 images drawn in crayon hanging on the wall behind my bed. I know now that at the time, Shane was really concerned, but instead of pointing out his concerns to me, Shane, casual as always, simply asked, "Hey, man! Whatcha doin'?" I laughed as I muttered something and became a little embarrassed. I put down the paper, and Shane and I proceeded to hang out.

Looking back on it now, although I was creating something, and creation is good, I was creating it with such malice and with such destruction that I created something negative and I was feeding off that energy. It finally culminated with an event that used to be the scariest thing that's ever happened in my life until recently. The images of what I'm about to describe are etched in my psyche, and I will never forget them and also never doubt that what I saw and experienced was real.

* * *

I was battling different "demons," as I call them. I don't think there is a clear verbiage to use, but that's what I'll call them now. There was one demon that was strongest, and I felt its presence most often. It is also the same one I am still battling today. I can just feel it. This figure was the one that would be hiding in the shadows across my room, or the one that would constantly move things or mess with the TV. It's the black figure I see out of the corner of my eye when no one else is there. It always liked to appear early in the morning, just before sunrise. One morning I woke, meaning my eyes opened, but I couldn't move my body. It was just beginning to get light outside, but the tint was still a pale blue. I looked across the room and there was an old woman on her hands and knees. Her face and skin were wrinkly and worn. Her eyes were black holes that sunk into her face. She was staring at me, waiting for me to see her. Once I did, she moved. She quickly crawled across the floor like a spider. I remember thinking as she crawled, this can't be real, this can't be real. Within seconds she was on top of me. I desperately tried to move my arms and legs to throw her off me, but I couldn't move. I could not move.

Her face was directly above mine, inches away from me. I saw a sense of pleasure on her face as she opened her mouth and put it over mine. Her mouth was as black as her eyes, and it began to suck something out of me. Not anything physical, but an energy—I could feel it. I could feel her sucking the life out of me. I struggled to move and was so scared. I tried wiggling and squirming, I wanted her to go away so badly. She wasn't pinning me down, but my body was paralyzed. I couldn't believe this was happening. Has there ever been a time where you had to hold your breath, say underwater, for just a *little* bit longer than you thought you could, and you get that panicky, "Holy shit, I might die!" moment? That's what I was experiencing. There was this physical thing right in front of me, but that's crazy, right? That can't happen? Only I felt it, I knew this was the same thing that had been haunting me for the last few months. I knew it like I know my son's name.

I don't know how, but I was able to finally move, I think the sheer will of not wanting to let her take me completely broke her grip on me, and once I felt my arm begin to move, I wildly shot up to my feet, waving my arms and screaming out in primal fear, and she was gone. I was more scared than I ever had been in my life. This was a real threat, and I knew if I didn't do something about it I was going to either be consumed by it and die or kill myself. I didn't go back to sleep; in fact, I didn't sleep much at all after that happened, so I watched movies. I remember trying to focus hard on the screen and not look over to the spot across my room where I had seen the old woman. The sun couldn't rise fast enough for me.

The only person I told about this and the only one who I thought would fully believe me was my sister, Lisa. She had always had a kind of interest in Wicca and tarot and things like that. I'll take a jab at her now and remind her of her goth days when she was in high school and always wore all black. I went to her house and told her very calmly and in detail what happened. She said it sounded like a succubus. When I described what the woman looked like and I then saw pictures of other people's descriptions and experiences of what a succubus is and what they look like, that fear came rushing back. This *was* real. I didn't imagine it, I was right, I saw it. And other people had experienced it too. I had no idea what it all meant, but I found comfort knowing I wasn't totally bat-shit crazy.

I told my sister the things I had been doing for the movie, and she about slapped me upside the head, asking me what the hell I was doing messing around with that shit? She said she had a friend who was much more knowledgeable than her and more capable of doing a clearing, and her name was Mary Chris. I paused because I didn't realize my sister was friends with my old music and computer teacher from elementary and grade school.

I'm ashamed of most things I did while a kid at school. Knowing now that I had bipolar disorder even back then but thought I was normal, I used to do a lot of things to gain the attention of the class at the emotional expense of others. I would always do things that were way more extreme than anyone else would do, and was also just plain mean. I remember once, I was in I think sixth grade, we were supposed to be starting music class, and we were all standing on the bleachers. There were only about 20 or 25 of us in the class. My friends and I were laughing because I had just done something horrible to our teacher. I think I probably wrote down that she was a bitch or ugly or something like that on a piece of paper, knowing that she'd read it.

She walked into the classroom, and we could all tell right away that something was not right. She burst into tears of frustration. She said that she was just trying to do the best she could to teach us kids. I remember feeling bad that I was the one who had brought on those tears, especially since I didn't have anything against her, but some of my bully friends did and I'd chime in on the dings, just to make them all laugh.

And now here I was 10 years later, hoping that she could help me. She and I have never talked about our relationship when we were teacher/student, but we have since established a great amount of respect for each other. When my mom retired as secretary of the church after 35 years or so, Mary Chris is the one who filled her position. I sent her an email saying how happy I was that she replaced my mom and that I know she will do an amazing job because she deeply cares for people and is a good person. I also thanked her for what she did for me.

It was night. My dad must have been out of town on business, which he often was, because I never would have risked him interrupting such a "ridiculous" thing. I opened the door and saw Mary Chris. I remember seeing a very serious expression on her face. She was there for business, which made me happy because I didn't know if she fully believed everything. I met with her at my sister's house prior to her coming over and told her all of the details so she had some idea what might be happening.

We went straight downstairs, and Mary Chris said to keep the lights off. She lit candles and put them on the edges of the pool table. I stood back in the corner where the fireplace is, kitty-corner from where I slept and where the old woman attacked me. I didn't say a word; I just watched. I watched as Mary Chris lit sage and went around the room speaking out. I wish I could remember what she was saying, but I don't. I was petrified, staring at the opposite corner of the room. I don't think my sister or Mary Chris could even see it if they wanted to, but it was there, the black figure, and it knew I brought help.

I could see it so vividly, just a dark, DARK mass in the corner, floating. Like a jellyfish floating in water, if that makes sense. The ritual wasn't more than 10 or 15 minutes, but as Mary Chris neared the end, the tone in the room changed. The candles went dim, but Mary Chris continued. I got nervous as I saw the black shape grow behind her. And then, with a rush of air and wind, the black mass went fleeing past me and outside the house. It couldn't be real, but everyone saw the candles blow as it left. I took a deep breath and looked around the room, and I'll be goddamned, but it was gone. It was like walking in sludge for three months and suddenly you're on asphalt.

I told Mary Chris that it was gone, I knew it. She said, "I know." She then warned me that she wasn't an all-powerful healer, and it could easily come back if I began to let it in again. This terrified me a bit, but I was confident to make a change. I SAW it leave ,so I was confident that it truly was gone. That was the week I went out and got Dutch.

* * *

Ask anyone who ever knew Dutch, and they'll all tell you that there was just something about him. Some animals just have a stronger, wiser, older energy in them, the same as people do. I felt safe when I was with Dutch. Every night, he was there. He became a witness to everything in my life. There was a time for a while where I was living a very unhealthy lifestyle. We had finished editing *black*. We were all super proud and pumped because we had finally edited together a story that flowed, and we thought was cool, and all the inserts worked perfectly, etc. There was one HUGE problem, though. Because we were so busy worrying about just getting all the shots, we made an entire movie without any production sound. For those not in the industry, this means that the only audio we had was from the camera mic, which is completely nowhere near okay for industry standards, and we had ludicrous delusions of grandeur that a Lionsgate or someone like that would pick up this movie. We had to do something.

So we searched for an audio engineer. We interviewed a few different ones and screened the movie for them. Looking back, I'm not sure why we didn't just drop off DVDs, but we were young and blindly ambitious. We had a bunch of local bands' music that made most scenes bearable, but there were other scenes where we would literally have to turn the volume all the way up on the TV just to hear what was going on and then quickly back down when a song or something would come on after it.

The last place we went to was a legit audio recording facility located in the loft of a building near the industrial district in Seattle. Not only did the sound guy, Brin, help do all the sound design, but he did the mixing, some scoring, and color correction. For all this, we were going to pay him $8,000. But Claude and I were both broke as shit, and so where the hell were we going to get that money from? I guess now is as good a time as any to introduce Donald. He'll continue to be a player later on in this story.

By this time, I had moved into an apartment on the outskirts of Seattle. If you wanted to go somewhere happening in the city, you had about 5 or 10 main options. One of these places was a two-story bar with a small dance floor, pool tables in the back, and karaoke every night, called Ozzie's. The place was always happening. When I first met Donald, I was working for my brother's company as a salesman, selling website designs to Harley-Davidson motorcycle dealerships. I was good at it, but I still hated it. It was a Monday to Friday, 9 to 5 gig. I didn't have a car so I would take the bus back to my apartment in Greenlake. Ozzie's was a block up and across the street from the building I worked at. More often than not, I would go sit at the bar and take the next bus. Sometimes that next bus would be at 1 in the morning.

Donald was a bartender there, and to this day he was one of the best bartenders I've ever seen. I became a regular and got to know Donald pretty well. I would get the same sandwich every time, and Donald would make sure I always had a fresh vodka/Red Bull in a pint glass. I began going there so often and tipping such large amounts that, before long, if Donald was working, I literally never had a tab. I would just give him a bunch of cash at the end or just have to pay for my food. It's nice when you're hooked up that well at a place like that. Makes it a lot easier to get girls—at least it did for me.

Over the next two years, Donald and I became very close, even though he and I had never hung out or even saw each other outside of Ozzie's. Until the day Claude and I, fresh off our meeting with Brin sat down at the bar with a deflated huff. By this time, Donald knew who Claude was and knew that we were making a movie. Matter of fact, we shot some inserts at Ozzie's for a scene in the movie where my character bumps into the femme fatale character, Alicia, and knocks the drink out of her hand and it smashes on the floor. Donald has always had an appreciation for pop culture and the arts and was very encouraging for us as filmmakers. He asked what was going on. I said casually, "Oh, nothing.

Just trying to figure out where to get $8,000." "What do you need it for?" "To basically redo all the sound and dialogue to fix the movie." "Well, I have eight grand," he said.

Claude's and my eyes lit up. The way Donald said it, it was like *why wouldn't you come to me in the first place?* Donald said he'd like to meet the guy and check out his place and talk about it, but no, eight grand was no problem for him. I couldn't believe it.

The first time I ever saw Donald outside the bar was at his aunt's coffee shop near Pike Place Market. We sat and talked about the movie and our plans for it. He said he'll give the dude four grand up front and the rest in monthly payments. It was going to take Brin two to three months to complete the work. Suddenly, Donald reached into his pocket and tossed a rolled-up wad of cash in my lap. "There you go. There's the four grand." Claude and I didn't know what to do. We thanked Donald, told him we'd see him later, and went down to Brin's and paid him. It was on.

* * *

It's hard for me to remember exactly what was going on when I think back upon that time. I was living a manic lifestyle but had not even a clue it was anything more than me just being busy. Of course, there was as much pleasure in my life as pain. I was going out as many nights as I could. I was raiding my dad's medicine cabinet and popping anything in my mouth that had a caution label on it. I was staying out late, going to work hungover and tired. I started taking these "caffeine" pills (speed) that would give me more energy than a can of energy drink. I was completely irresponsible in every aspect of everything I was doing, including having a dog.

I joke about it now, but I should not own a dog. Kids, fine. Dogs, no. I got one more dog I'll tell you about later, and he's just as fucked up as Dutch was, but what Dutch did have was a staunch individuality. Dutch would always get into something when I would leave to go out partying at night. My dad would be out of town and I'd leave Dutch alone in the house, and he'd end up tearing up a couch cushion, peeing somewhere, shitting somewhere else, or getting into the trash. Most nights it was all four.

I don't know if it's the bipolar, I know drinking doesn't help it, but I have a bit of a temper. Anyone that's ever seen it in action will agree. It breaks my heart writing this, but it's the truth. I used to beat the fucking shit out of Dutch when I would come home piss drunk and see that he got into the trash again. Dutch knew he was in for an ass-whooping too. He'd just lie there on the ground with his head down. I'd slap him harder than I knew I should and shove his face into the garbage and kick him in the side.

But no matter what, he'd end up curled up with me a half-hour later with me apologizing to him. I can only imagine how all of my ex-girlfriends dealt with me. From my incredible extremes of excessive anger and violence to five minutes later wanting to be loved and charming and acting as if nothing happened. There's a reason I chose to write this book. One of them is to try and find that line *between* the manic and the creative. Back then, I only thought it was one: the creative. But this dog, this black angel of a dog, took every outburst, every punch, every kick—he never blamed me for any of it. It's as if he knew more about me than I knew myself. I'm not sure if he put up with it because that was just him, but I now believe in my heart of hearts that Dutch's sole purpose throughout his life was to be there for me. If not for Dutch, I'm pretty sure I would have killed myself. Period.

I remember I had come home one night from going out. My dad was out of town again and I was pissed at Dutch's most recent pillow thrashing. So I thought I'd put him in the bathroom downstairs and close the door. I took out the trash, the rugs, I put the light on with some of his toys and food and water. The floors were linoleum, so it would be easy to clean up if he peed in there; I thought it was a good idea.

I came home late, as usual. As soon as I walked inside the house upstairs, I could hear Dutch barking down below. That kind of high-pitched bark he'd do when he didn't like something. It sounded like he'd been doing it for hours. I quickly turned on some lights and ran downstairs. I immediately began apologizing for leaving him in there and went to open the door, only it was locked. The button to lock the door was on the inside. Dutch had been clawing and jumping at the door the entire time, and he'd hit the button to lock the door. I panicked.

It took me about two seconds to make up my decision. I leaned my shoulder down and broke the lock on the door. Wood went splintering everywhere. My heart quickly sank with the guilt of having to explain such irresponsibility to my dad, but that quickly went away when Dutch jumped on his hind legs and started licking my face, tail wagging fiercely. I told him how sorry I was, took him for a walk, super-glued the wood back in place so my dad wouldn't find out for at least a couple weeks, and then went and watched a movie with Dutch in bed. Guess which one?

"More of a pillar, I will never know.

You burdened a castle of pain, so I could grow.

A life not wasted.

Not a moment forgotten.

Live life to the extreme and see what it is you were meant for."

CHAPTER TWO: GOING TO CALIFORNIA

I was standing by the front door of the same house where I had experienced the most horrific experience of my life to date that I spoke about in the previous chapter. I think my mom was the one waiting outside to give me a ride to SeaTac Airport. Actually, it could have been Sara, my recently discovered new girlfriend. *black* was finished and was playing at a film festival in LA. A shitty, no-name festival that we had to pay to get in to and that doesn't exist today, but it was accepted. I gave my dad a hug and looked around to make sure I had everything. All set. There was only one thing left to do and that was say goodbye to Dutch. The place I was moving into allowed pets, but I was too irresponsible to take him with me.

I had thought I would be okay with leaving Dutch, but I never cried like I did with him then. I remember bending down, and he rolled over on his back. I embraced him like I would my brother and I completely lost it. I remember a fleeting second of embarrassment because my dad had never seen me cry like this before—no one had really. As I sobbed, I whispered into his ears that I would come back for him, I loved him, and I would miss him dearly. This is another prime example of why I should never own a dog.

Most everyone else I know would have taken into consideration the fact that they had a dog when moving over a thousand miles away, but not me. I had a couple hundred bucks to my name, I was *flying* down to LA, and the apartment I was staying at *may* have let dogs there, but I didn't know because I didn't even ask. It was easier for me to leave him with my dad and not take the extra responsibility. Goddamn, I used to be so selfish. It's still a fault of mine today, but I am at least aware of it now and trying to change that. Back then, I would tell myself anything in order to not feel bad for being a piece of shit.

I will say this, at that moment, I felt as if I was leaving part of me behind. I didn't realize just how big of a hole in my heart that dog filled for me. I wish I could have been inside that dog's brain sometimes and at times I felt like I was. He knew I was sad but probably had no idea why or when he'd ever see me again, if ever. I, of course, had plans to get my feet under me and make money and then bring Dutch down to live as soon as I could. Little did I know, it would be years and much more heartache for me before finally bringing him down to live with me in California.

I don't remember much after that. My next memory is standing outside the Burbank airport with a massive duffle bag and a huge box taped together with my computer and other things inside. This was everything. I was 25. Let me jump back a few months and give you some context.

Like I said, *black* was done. It was summer, and I was trying to plan my next move now that I had a completed feature film under my belt. I talked to my mom one day, and she told me she ran into someone I went to high school with named David at church. He was a year ahead of me, not grossly popular, kind of weird, but I knew who she was talking about, and apparently he remembered who I was too. My mom asked him what he had been up to since high school and he told her that he lived in LA with his brother and they worked in movies. That's all I knew. My mom told him that I had just finished making a movie and he gave her his number for me to call.

I remember sitting in my dad's office downstairs and calling David. He was a lot more receptive to the call than I had thought. He asked how my brother was doing and so on and then began asking about my movie. I told him all about it and he said he'd love to see it. Nowadays, I would have just uploaded that thing to Vimeo, slapped a passcode on it, and it would all be good. But instead, I decided to hop on a plane with Claude, the director, and we'd pay him a visit down in LA. I knew one other girl I went to school with from the Art Institute of Seattle who lived down there. She and I had fooled around a few times and Claude also knew her from school so we decided to stay with her.

So Claude and I set up a meeting with David and arranged enough time for him to watch our movie, and we flew down to LA. We flew into LAX. We had no money, no car, no rental. David's office was in Universal City, so we took the "train/subway" from LAX to try and get up there. Talk about a stranger in a strange land. The train took us through south LA and then up north and eventually east toward Universal. It was like a two to three-hour commute for us, and we had absolutely no fucking clue where we were. Claude was used to navigating big cities like New York and Paris and so he pretty much navigated us.

We eventually made it to David's office. If you ever drive south on the 101 right after the 134 split and there's that really tall building standing alone on the left side with "Universal" at the top, that's where David's office was. Claude and I had to check in with security and get name badges. We were stoked when we found out David had put our names on the list. He was expecting us. This was my first Hollywood meeting, and I thought I was big time. We went up to some floor in the middle and were met by David. Right away, any weirdness went away, as he didn't look like the kid I remembered from high school. He was dressed business casual, had his face shaved, and treated us very professionally.

We went into a conference room that had a TV and DVD player set up in it and we played *black* for him. Looking back on it now, there's no fucking way in hell that anyone would take a meeting and sit and watch the entire movie in their office. It just doesn't happen. Sure, maybe he was just being nice, but knowing what I know now, there was absolutely nothing that David could do for us. But at the time, I thought this was it. My dad even had warned me, "If he tries to offer you something right there, no matter what, say no. Don't sign anything. He might try and screw you." My dad's paranoia and precaution would go on for the next several years until I finally realized I know way more about this business

...han he ever will and stopped listening to him. My dad does understand the art of business ...nd negotiating in general; I'm just too impatient to ever fully heed his advice.

David took us out for tacos after that and then had to get back to the office. Claude ...nd I were going to putt around Universal City for a while until our friend from the Art ...nstitute could come and pick us up. It was April, and *Dawn of the Dead* was out in theaters. ...laude and I decided to go see it. It was one of the most memorable movie-going ...xperiences of my life. Not only is the film near perfect (Zack Snyder's best film by far) but I ...emember thinking the entire time, this is what I want to be doing with my life. I *need* to be ...aking movies. The movie ended, and Claude and I walked outside. I can remember it ...ividly, looking around at all the sights and sounds of the Universal Citywalk, the clear blue ...kies, the warm weather...I turned and looked at Claude and said, "I'm moving here." Fast-...orward four months, and there I was.

* * *

I'm not sure of where to go next. Let me just sum up the next few months of my life ...ith a bunch of stories that every person who's ever lived in LA and tried to make it in the ...ntertainment business have. These are all 100% true.

The first job I got was off a craigslist ad. I didn't know really what it was for, all I ...new was that it involved sales, and I'm a great salesman. I got an interview set up and so I ...ut on my best slacks, shirt, and tie and walked up to Sunset Blvd. near the Chinese ...heater. When I walked into the office, I was told to sit in a waiting room with about 15 to ...0 other kids all my age, only none of them were wearing a tie. None of them were even ...earing dress shoes; they were all just wearing their regular clothing. I remember thinking ...o myself, how unprofessional! Have none of these people ever gone in for an interview? ...hen, the owner came out and I discovered there was no interview process—just by ...howing up, we all already had the job.

The owner dressed well, with slicked-back hair and a shiny watch. As he made his ...ntroduction and told us about the "training" we were going to do that day, I noticed his ...attoos on his neck and face. I've known friends who had similar tattoos, and I knew what ...hey meant and where he got them. I don't think anyone else in the room picked up on it. ...robably not, since they were all wannabe actors/writers/whatever as well and looked like ...hey'd never seen the tail end of a fist coming at their face. But I could be wrong.

What the job was, and if there are still companies that are able to function today by ...roviding this same "service," then they should all be destroyed. It was a "talent agency" ...hat provided a database of clients to casting directors, producers, commercial directors, ...tc. The leads we got were solid. People in bum-fuck Ohio or somewhere (sorry, Ohio) filled out their information on the company's website and would request to know more. Each salesperson was assigned a different area of the country and would call the leads from those various "offices." We then would convince these kids that if they signed up for our service, we'd send their headshots around and get them auditions and blah, blah, blah. It was a complete fucking scam, but I was good at it.

The first call I made, the very first one, I made a sale. It was that easy. Sometimes the kid who submitted their info would be young, and their parent would get on the phone and call you out for being a scam, but I'm really good on the phone and would sometimes not only convert their kids but sometimes the moms too. There was no punch-in or time clocks or anything like that, and we were paid cash at the end of every day for any sales made, and a weekly paycheck that could only be cashed at some small-ass bank I'd never heard of that was across the street. But it was a job!

* * *

Everyone in LA has a story about the time someone took nude or revealing photos in a promise that it would help further their career. If they don't, they're either full of shit or they haven't lived in LA long enough. This is my story of that.

I met this dude through some of my neighbors that you would swear was gayer than a kitten on catnip, but he VEHEMENTLY denied any such allegations, which just made it more confusing and/or obvious. But he got me a job running sales and marketing for *The Ten Commandments: The Musical*, starring Val Kilmer as Moses. Yes, that was a real production, and it was a fucking INCREDIBLE show. Google it.

So this guy wasn't completely full of shit. He was a manager for Curly Sue in the musical and partied with Val a lot. He lived in this huge house up on Sunset Plaza, so I figured the guy had to have *some* legitimacy and connections. I would hang out a lot at his house on my days off. He lived the Hollywood lifestyle I so desperately wanted that it felt good to be around all the action, even if 99% of it was bullshit. He would throw me some cash here and there, and he always had booze to drink at his house.

One day, he said he got an email from a client looking for an underwear model, male. I had done *some* modeling in Seattle and he told me the payday was $10,000. He would take his 15% for manager fee, but that amount of money at that time was life-changing for me. The guy (I forget what his name was) asked if I had any headshots or body shots. "Not really," I said. He then suggested we take some photos there at his house in my underwear and submit them. He said he felt just as awkward to take the pictures as I was to be in them only wearing my underwear, but I kept thinking about that ten grand.

He told me the client wanted an All-American look. I'm about as All-American looking as can be, but he thought we should drape an American flag over my shoulders, so we did. Then he thought it'd be cute if I posed with the flag and holding his little Yorkie, so we did. He took about 30 or so pictures from his digital camera. He let me see them, saying how weird he felt the whole time. I felt weird as well, but I had done it, so what the hell, right? So, somewhere out there, there are photos of me wearing nothing but white Hanes underwear, with an American flag draped over my shoulders and holding a tiny dog. If you ever come across them, send them to me. I would love the laugh.

As I was thinking again about this story and retelling it just now, another memory popped into my head. I would sometimes crash at this guy's house after a night of partying. I usually slept on the couch, but one night someone else was crashing there too so he told me to crash in his bed with him. It was a big enough bed. I've shared a bed with my brother before or my best friends, but I had only known this guy a couple months and still didn't have him all the way figured out. But it's not like I was afraid of him. He acted like such a pussy, and I was way bigger and more intimidating than him, so I shared the bed with him. The weird part is that he put on a porn movie to fall asleep to. There was no way I was going to fall asleep before he did. So I forced myself to stay up and awake until he fell asleep. I finally passed out, and when I woke up the next day, he was already up and brewing coffee. I'm pretty sure that's the last time I crashed at his house.

* * *

The year I moved to Los Angeles happened to be the same year of the most rain the city's ever had since they began recording rainfall in the 1800s. This city isn't equipped for that much rain, and everything flooded. I didn't have a car and walked everywhere. Being from Seattle, it didn't bother me much at all. If it were to rain that much now, I'd hate my life (even though we could use the water). The roommate I had was moving and I couldn't afford the place on my own, so David offered me to stay at his place. He rarely stayed there, so it would pretty much be my own. It was a 250-square-foot studio apartment, and if I stretched, I could scramble eggs and take a shower at the same time. But it was cheap. Like, $300 a month cheap.

The building was off of Santa Monica Blvd. and Formosa Ave., a few blocks down from my favorite bar/restaurant in LA, Jones Café. David had gotten me a job at his and his brother's post-production studio as studio manager. I loved it. Even though there wasn't a whole heck of a lot to do, I got to wake up every day and go to work in the business. I felt settled in for the first time in LA, and it was the first time I thought about Dutch and wanted him to be down there with me. The place was small, but Dutch and I have lived in small spaces before. There was a stint back during the Art Institute days where my dad and I got into a huge fight and I left and lived in my sister's basement for a while. The ceiling was so low that there wasn't a single place in there where I could stand tall fully.

I asked David if I could bring my dog down and stay there. He was reluctant and said it probably wasn't a great idea. He had some sort of "in" with the landlord and didn't want to disrupt that. I respected it. That building was filled with all sorts of characters, and the landlord knew it. He didn't say much as long as rent was paid on time. I was getting paid $500/week, and my expenses were minimal, but because I fucking suck with money, I was always broke. As I write this, I still fucking suck with money and I'm still broke.

It's foggy why exactly, but that girl, Sara, I had met just before I left for LA and I stayed together. We fell in love, and she would come for visits. Although I don't remember her specifically convincing me to give up on LA for a while and move back to Seattle, I think I just took the easier path. I would live with Sara, and then we'd eventually come back down to LA together and I would continue my dreams of making movies. She worked in real estate, and she even interviewed at a few places down here when she would come and visit. It was a dumb fucking decision, and I never should have left, but had I stayed, I'm confident that not only would I not be broke right now but I also wouldn't be married to my wife, I wouldn't have my beautiful son, I wouldn't have the amazing house we live in today, and I'd still be a piece of shit. It's funny how things work out that way.

* * *

I want to break off for a second and tell you that all of the girlfriends I've ever had all taught me something. Whether that something was good or bad, that was for me to define. But I want no ill will toward any of them. I can only imagine being with someone who is manic and bipolar and not knowing it and having to deal with that. Some of them handled it better than others, and I definitely manipulated them, or at least tried to, more often than not. I just wanted to get that out there.

* * *

So I left LA and went back to Seattle. I had arranged for a job before I moved back, working at KISW, the local rock radio station, as a promo person. I convinced Sara to let Dutch stay with us in her apartment, even though we had to hide me and Dutch from the landlord. By this time, Donald was now working as a GM for Hooters restaurants, running the Seattle store. He got me a job as a line cook at his restaurant, and within a month or two, I was an assistant manager. Sara wasn't too fond of me hanging out with 18- and 19-year-old girls (she was seven years older than me), and it wasn't long before she and I were through. Funny story…

I had known for about a month that I was over Sara and we needed to break up. I don't remember exactly what the argument was over, but I just remember Sara going off about something and I said we're done. She told me to get my shit and get the fuck out of her place and stormed out the front door. A few seconds later, she came back in and looked around the place. She saw a picture on the wall—it must have been of the two of us—and she smashed it on the countertop and then said, "There! Now I feel better!" and she left. I called Donald and was like, "Dude, you gotta come get me. Bitch has gone crazy!" Donald was there in 20 minutes and helped me pack up my things and go.

By this time, I was making a decent salary, but I didn't have enough money for a full deposit plus first month's rent. Donald loaned me the cash through the store, and I paid it off. I moved into a nice, big apartment complex. I lived in a 550-square-foot studio, but it felt like I was living like a king. The best part about it? Dutch and I were on our own again, just the way we liked it. We didn't have to hide him from the landlord. The exit door was right next to my apartment so I could take him outside and for walks easily and without much complication. I was making money and paying rent on time—life was really good. I miss those days and that apartment.

Three months after starting work in the restaurant business, I was promoted to general manager of my own location in Lynnwood, Washington. It's the neighboring town of my hometown, Everett, so I was very familiar with the area and the people. With the promotion came a yearly salary of $54,000 a year plus bonuses. It was the most money I had ever made in a year—still is. My lease was up, and there was a large one-bedroom apartment in my building opening up above me that had a deck and was way bigger. I took it. I wish I hadn't. But like so many other things that have happened in my life, I'm not sure if I was ever fully in control of steering the ship. I believe the Universe has woven my life through a series of events to led me to where I am today.

The next two years of my life aren't necessarily a blur, and they were filled with a bunch of shit that happened. I fell in love with a drug addict. My friendship with Donald grew. I also became close with Owen. He was a cook at Ozzie's, and when Donald moved to Hooters restaurants, he brought Owen along as a line cook. I partied a LOT. I can think of several times I should have been killed or put in jail. I fell in love again with a girl I thought I was going to marry, and I eventually got fired from my job, and my girlfriend and I moved to the East Bay area of northern California, so a lot happened. But instead of going into any great detail about those events, I'll tell you three stories that involve Dutch so you can find out just what an asshole he really was. Two of them involve my best friend, Shane. Shane is still my closest friend to this day; I no longer talk to Donald or Owen.

* * *

Shane would often come to Seattle to visit ,and we would go out on the town drinking. Shane is the most responsible person I know, and there were probably a dozen or more times that because of his responsibility, I didn't do something too fucking stupid. One night, we ordered pizza at my house before we went out. It was an extra-large from Papa John's. We each had a couple of pieces and then were going to save the rest of it, say 60%, for when we got home from the bars and would enjoy it in our drunken stupor.

The box wouldn't fit in the fridge properly so I put it high up on the counter as far back as I could and Shane and I went out on the town. It's pretty impossible for Shane and I ever to not have a good night together. We just click so unbelievably well—we literally could sit and watch *Family Guy* for hours and do nothing but bullshit about *Seinfeld*-esque topics. It's why we love road-tripping together so much. My point is, I don't remember what we specifically did that night, you'd have to ask him. (He also has the greatest fucking memory ever! He remembers every little detail). But I remember when Shane and I came back to my apartment laughing about something, ready to destroy the rest of that pizza. When I opened the door and turned the corner we saw the box on the kitchen floor and not a speck of pizza to be found anywhere. We looked over in the living room and there was Dutch lying on the ground with his head down. I was in such shock that he ate the entire fucking pizza that I couldn't beat the shit out of him; it was just too classic of a Dutch move. Shane was so pissed—he was talking about that pizza the whole ride home from the bars that night.

Another night, it could have been the same one, Shane was asleep on my couch and I was asleep in my bedroom. Shane told me the next morning what Dutch did while he was sleeping on the couch. Sometime around 3 or 4 in the morning, Shane woke up to Dutch walking into the living room. Dutch looked at Shane as he walked up to him and stopped. Dutch then peed like a water hose on the rug. In case you're trying to picture the visuals, I do have to say that Dutch never peed like a regular boy dog, he peed like a girl dog. Dutch maybe peed like a boy dog three times in his life; I never got it. Anyway, there was Dutch, peeing like a girl in the middle of the living room. He streamed for about 30 seconds or so and then turned around and went back into my bedroom. I can't stop chuckling as I write this now remembering how much of a complete dickhead Dutch was. Makes me laugh.

This next story may have happened during this time period as well—either way it's super gross and you have to hear it. My mom was watching Dutch for some reason. I may have been out of town or I don't know. My mom was living in a nice house in a good neighborhood in Marysville, just north of Everett. She had a decent backyard with a fence that went around both sides of the house, so there was plenty of room for dogs to run. She had let Dutch outside to go pee or whatever, and he spotted something in the grass and immediately pounced on it. My mom yelled out for him, but it was too late. Dutch turned around, and my mom saw a snake tail whipping back and forth out of Dutch's mouth. My mom got super grossed out, as any human being would, and he proceeded to eat the snake live and whole.

I'll close with one of my favorite memories of him during this time. The drug addict I was dating was always gone, not answering her phone, giving excuses, etc. It was a Sunday and she was going to go hang out with her friends at this waterfall. I had the day off and wanted to hang out with her. She said she'd be back around like 2 or 3 in the afternoon. I said cool. She left early in the morning ,and I didn't feel like doing shit, so Dutch and I decided to stay in bed and start watching *Band of Brothers*. It's like a 10-disc set or something like that. We watched the first episode, and I was completely hooked and started to binge the entire season on DVD.

Well, 3:00 PM rolled by and still no word from my girlfriend. Of course, I called and texted, but got no response. 3:00 became 5:00, 5:00 became 8:00, 8:00 became the next day. I had a really hard time fighting off jealous feelings. I knew what she was doing and who she was hanging out with, and they were, and most likely still are, complete fucking losers. I wanted any possible excuse or reason to beat the living shit out of this one pussy-ass bitch who was dealing her oxy. And whether Dutch knew it or not, I feel like he had a pretty good read on me, so chances are he did it on purpose, but every time I was feeling angry or jealous, Dutch would just put his head on my lap. We watched the entire season of *Band of Brothers*, drank some beer, ate some pizza...it was one of the best days I've ever had with that dog. Goddamn, he was such an incredible dog to me.

* * *

So we were headed to California, this time with my girlfriend, Shauna, and Dutch in tow. Donald and Owen had been down in the East Bay area for a few months now and were working for a different Hooters franchise. The plan was that I was going to be assistant general manager for Donald for a year, save up money, and then Blondie and I would move to LA and I would restart my dreams of making movies once again. That plan worked—sort of. When I look back on that year, I feel like I was super-focused. When I sat with the franchise owner for my interview, I was very honest that I was only there for a year but that I would be the greatest fucking manager he'd ever had during that year, and he was down with that plan. So having an end game already in place, I didn't feel stuck like I did in Seattle. Plus, the weather was INCREDIBLE. It was always hot and sunny. We had a pool in our apartment complex, I started running again, and life was good.

A couple months before we were set to move, I could sense something off between Blondie and I. I remember we sat down at my kitchen table, and I asked her if she was still on board with the plan of us moving to LA in a few months, and she said no, not really. I said okay, I guess this is it then. Movies were, and always have been, my life, and I wouldn't sacrifice giving up on them for anyone. Now, looking back on our situation and knowing that I had the bipolar in me the whole time, I can remember numerous fights we had where I probably came off as a complete psychopath, but in my head I was being completely rational. She has witnessed the worst of me.

Plans also changed with Donald. I hinted at it before, but he had/has a love for attention and "celebrity," at least he did heavily during this point in his life. When the time grew close for me to move to LA (I had already been driving down occasionally, taking some meetings), Donald started not giving a shit about his job anymore. He started looking at houses around Hollywood and wanted to move down with me. Owen, the lemming he is, was going to follow blindly as well. Oh, and Donald's girlfriend too. On the one hand, I was excited. Donald was looking at houses in the hills. We thought we were going to go down there and be the new *Entourage*. Seriously, I was the Vince of the group, we had our Drama, we had our Turtle, and Donald was my E. On the other hand, it was us living together that ruined our friendship for good.

I speak of it a lot now in all of my content, and the reason I'm so confident when I say, "the alluring curtain" of Hollywood, is because I lived it. It's unbelievably easy to be sucked into the Hollywood machine and "apparent" lifestyle. It is why so many people in this city have turned to drugs, or violence, or given up and left, or just committed suicide. I want to stand firm and clear: the entertainment industry is the most disgusting industry I have ever come across. It is filled with lies and fake promises but presented to you on a silver platter with blue skies, sunshine, bikinis, and palm trees. This is why I want to destroy it. I want to hit the reset button on Hollywood just like the reset button was hit for me in life. There will be carnage, there will be pain, there will be confusion. But what remains for all of us on the other side will make everyone be a better human being, and I believe that is important right now.

"Friends come easy,

Friends come neat.

A friend in life is what they are when you need it.

Once you realize your importance to others, you can understand your own importance to yourself."

CHAPTER THREE: HOLLYWOOD UNDEAD

The house Donald had decided on was above Fremont Ave. in the Hollywood Hills, near my second favorite bar/restaurant in LA called Birds. The address was 5537 Tuxedo Terrace. The street name couldn't have been more fitting. I can't remember why, but Owen and I had to load up the entire U-Haul. It was a pain in the ass—we were super unprepared, I stayed up far later than I should have, but we got up, later than planned, the next day and made the trip down. I think Donald went down there a day or two before. To be honest, I really don't know why he left us to pack everything up, and Owen and I bitched to each other about it. Anyway, I drove down from the Bay Area in my Jeep with all my things packed up, including Dutch. Owen and I left together, but he was forced to drive the massive U-Haul along with his car being towed on a trailer, so we arrived at different times. I'm glad I didn't have to drive it.

I was the first to arrive. I couldn't believe we were going to live in this huge place in comparison to any other place I had lived in as an adult. It was two stories, with a rock garden in the center of the staircase, a back patio with a ping-pong table, garage, chimney, and a large living room area with high ceilings. Donald paid the deposit and first and last months' rent all on his own. After we signed the paperwork, we poured a shot and toasted to all of us being down in Hollywood and to all the great things that were to come. We had drunk the Kool-Aid.

I remember feeling right at home again. To this day, Hollywood is still one of my favorite parts of LA. I was finally back where I belonged after being away for so many years. I was single, I had my friends, and I started to get to work. I began pounding the pavement, trying to get an agent, trying to get modeling gigs, anything I could think of to help me in my career. What I *should* have done, and my advice to anyone who moves to LA to pursue a career in the entertainment industry now, is to get a job right away and don't worry about anything else. Time is the key to surviving LA. Time and patience. I possessed neither. I was expecting to quickly catapult my way into the industry somehow, even though nobody knew who the hell I was and my resume was for shit. I *had* written and produced a feature-length film already, so among my peers, I was ahead of the game. I began writing some more, because I only had one or two finished screenplays at the time. I haven't opened up those scripts in a number of years because I know just how bad they are. But at the time I thought they were winners.

Donald was the first to gain employment. He interviewed and was later hired as GM for a Mexican joint in the marina that had been around for 35 years called Baja Cantina. It wasn't long before Owen began working there, and eventually Donald got me hired on the staff as well. This is the point in my story where I'd like to introduce you to the greatest person I will ever know and the mother of my child, Abigail Richie. I'd like to tell you all a quick story about the first time Abi saw me walk into Baja for the first time. It makes me smile when I hear her tell the story to others. I was the exact personification of everything she hated in a dude, yet we still ended up together. It makes me laugh every time.

I think I had a goatee. I know I had recently shaved my head, because before I was rocking a Mohawk and obviously couldn't have that style of hair as a server there. I can show you all pictures of what I look like with a shaved head and a goatee, but take my word for it, I look like the biggest fucking douchebag you've ever met. It was the same look I rocked back in high school. It took a really great woman to teach me how to dress and look, even though I still go through my crazy periods. Anyway, Abi was working that day and she would later tell me that when I first walked in, she was literally saying to the other staff, "Where the fuck are they finding these douchebags?!" Needless to say, she was not thrilled. Nor were much of the staff. They had all been there for years, and the "cocktail mafia" as it became known to me, ran the place. Donald came from a corporate restaurant mind-set, with all his personality and ego, and immediately began to make changes that upset the mafia. For some reason, Donald didn't want anyone there to know that we not only lived together but had known each other for years.

I was always loyal to Donald and always took his side, but there are two sides to every situation. The more I got to know the cocktail girls, the more I understood that they were actually the reason the restaurant was so busy and packed all the time. Donald's personality, at least back then, was the kind that was difficult to get him to change his opinion. He was very firm in his decisions, and while he was great at weeding out the employees who sucked or just didn't fit in, he replaced them with incoherent morons. He didn't give the due respect, positivity, and accolades that the five to six core employees ever deserved. Thinking back on it now and observing it from the outside, it was pretty obvious to me that Donald enjoyed being at the top and being the best/most liked/etc. Deep down he knew that his aces always ran the show—the unfortunate thing is that he would never admit it. I didn't struggle with that humbleness.

* * *

About four or five months after we had moved, Donald and his new girlfriend who had driven down with us broke up. Donald was depressed, and so I convinced him that we should go to the dog shelter and he should get a dog. It would help cheer him up, I thought. I regret that decision.

Donald and I went to a shelter near Compton to look at what they had. Same as before when I found Dutch, we were looking for a "dog"-like dog. There were some I thought would be cool if he got, like an old curly-haired dog, but he probably only had a few more years left in him. Then, we came across a litter of puppies. They were a pit bull mix, with tan short hair, and were absolutely adorable. Well, not only did Donald decide on one of these, but I was suckered into getting my second dog, Hauser.

Funny story...Donald and I both wanted boy dogs. Donald picked his out and I picked out mine. Out of all these puppies, they were all super chill and sleeping and being nice. Those were the ones Donald and I wanted. There was one puppy, however, who was climbing over the rest of them, biting their tails and their ears.

When we went to tell the lady at the shelter which dogs we had both picked out, she said that Donald's was available but that I'd have to pick a different one because someone else had already reserved the one I chose. I went back to the kennel and looked, and the only other male dog left was that jackass who was climbing over everyone else and biting them. So I picked him. Again, I'm saying it was a bad decision. As I've said before, I shouldn't be allowed to own a dog, let alone two of them. But I will say this: I still have Hauser and he and I have since developed an understandable relationship that I think will only grow better in time, what left he has of it. Donald got rid of his dog within less than a year.

These new dogs were straight-up puppies. Mix that with a bunch of dudes who don't care much about mess and don't know how to properly care for a dog, and you get what we started getting on a daily basis: piss and shit everywhere in the house. And because Dutch is a dick like that, he began peeing and shitting inside the house as well because, well, why not? He saw the puppies doing it, so he was like "fuck it."

Donald's dog began staying in my room, which was annoying because it was supposed to be his dog, but I could understand because his litter brother, Hauser, was in there with me. Also, Dutch took an immediate liking and protective attitude toward Hauser, which made me happy. However, I once again began leaving them alone in my room when I would go to work, and I would return home to piles of shit in my room and the carpet ripped to shreds. None of us were very responsible in that house when it came to the integrity of it. There was only so much we could hide before the landlords found out that we had gotten two more dogs, and they were puppies and the entire house was carpeted, so they were ripping it to shreds. These were definitely the beginning factors to the demise of the friendship between Donald and myself.

The first thing that caused so much friction was I hadn't been paying any rent early on. I paid for cable, Internet, phone, things like that, but it was Donald who wanted the $3,500/month rent so we could look like we were ballers and live in a big house up in the hills, but I would have been fine moving back into my 250-square-foot studio apartment. I told him I couldn't afford the rent before we moved down, and he said don't worry about it. Again, I was the Vinny Chase to his E. But reality began to set in for both of us, and it was causing major unspoken friction. I wasn't "killing it" yet in the movie industry, and Donald as getting tired of paying for everything. I also think he was hemorrhaging more money than he was taking in, and that fucked with him too. I had never known Donald to not have or not be worried about money, ever. He was now, and I think that's a big reason we began to part ways.

This was the first time in a while where I was no longer on the management side of things with Donald; instead, I was just an employee. What happens when you're just an employee? You hear all the other employees talk shit about the boss, which is what started happening at Baja Cantina. Donald was considered the enemy. The fact that most all of them still didn't know that Donald and I lived together was weird. Donald would make shit up like that all the time and I never understood why; I just rolled with it. So I started hanging out with the other staff and hanging out on the block more so that caused some separation as well.

In the end, I don't think Donald and I could have remained friends much longer. We were both headed in such different directions that it was only a matter of time. I think the final nail in the coffin was when I told him about Abi and that she was going up to Seattle with me for Thanksgiving. I had fallen completely head over heels in love with Abigail and I still am. Our relationship has changed over the years, but we still deeply care for one another.

* * *

I already told you what Abi thought of me the first time she saw me. I remember the first time I saw her. Abi had really short hair when I first met her. Apparently, she'd never had short hair before and it was always long and she had just cut it all off. I think she just got back from a vacation as well. All of her female co-workers were saying how much they liked it. She got my attention. Not because I thought she was attractive by any means, which sounds completely absurd saying that now, because I don't think I'll ever be fortunate enough to meet a more beautiful woman, but it just showed me that okay, people around here like this girl and she's probably pretty cool.

I was working, and Abi came in and I overheard her say that she just got her first agent. I didn't know what for. Then I saw some modeling pictures she had, and I was impressed. This girl looks good in front of a camera; still, there was no attraction. It was then that we discovered we both wanted to be in the movie business, she an actor, myself a writer. It's a good thing I got really good at writing, because I gave her my "best" script I had at the time and I thought it was amazing, but it was just shit and she thought so too. Still no attraction.

Abi and I began working a lot of the same shifts together, mostly days. They were fairly quiet, and we started bullshitting back and forth with each other. It was much more of a friendship still. I was "dating" a few different girls back and forth, and Abi just never showed up on my radar. We were working one shift together and I was at the back bar and she was cocktailing in the section near the back. I had to go up to the front bar to grab something and as I walked back through the crowd toward my bar, I saw Abi walking in front of me. All of the cocktailers there wore black leggings. I had to take the opportunity to check out Abi's ass and I remember saying to myself, oh! She's *not* fat. She's actually got a banging little body. For some reason, I had pegged her as not having a great body. Boy, was I wrong. Hmm...good for her. Still no attraction.

We were working Fourth of July. Baja fences off their parking lot and does a big party with a stage and music and outside bars—at least they did at the time. Abi and I were working at two of the different bars outside. We didn't have to wear our usual uniform that day, as long as we wore red, white, and blue. The day was just getting started, and the girls were all complimenting each other on their cute outfits. The girls, of course, all wore bikini tops and jeans shorts or things of that nature. Then, I don't remember who it was, I overheard one of the male co-workers talking about Abi's boobs and how he had no idea they were so big. I had to investigate for myself. I walked over to the bar she was at. She was working with Madison, an absolutely stunningly beautiful woman. I went up and looked at Abi's bikini and thought holy shit! She's got real big boobs! Still no attraction.

One day as I was making drinks for Abi behind the bar and as she was waiting for me to make them, she put her foot under the well and tapped the end of her shoed toes on my crotch. I was so shocked. I looked up at her face and it was just a deadpan: "What?" Anyone who knows Abi knows she just has this amazing comedic timing, super dry and witty. She's a lot funnier than I am. So, we began this game of her always tapping my crotch with her foot. I began to like it. I also began noticing her feet more. Abi has perfect feet. Attraction was building....

I was standing at the back bar, and in usual Ryan fashion, I was flirting with Madison, probably telling her how gorgeous our babies would be. Not only did Madison have a boyfriend she'd been with for years, but I don't think I'm her type. She was laughing and said something, and when she said it, I'm being dead serious, something in my brain clicked over. Maddy said, "Oh, Ryan...you know you'd have a better chance of getting with Abi than me." Game Over. I literally turned around, walked straight up to the front bar, and immediately began flirting with Abi. Just like that, I had switched her over in my head from friend to mate. It was really, really weird.

Anyways, Abi stepped up her flirtation game as well, and before we knew it, we both were attracted to the other and desperately wanted to hook up. But there was no way in hell we were going to let anyone else know about it. I mean, *Ryan and Abi???* It almost made us disgusted at the thought, so there's no way anyone else would understand. So we had to be secret, and secret we were. It finally built up to our first kiss.

* * *

It was Halloween. We nearly had our first kiss two nights before, but we just missed it on the timing. We knew the next shift we worked together it was going to happen right after. Abi worked earlier in the day, and I wasn't supposed to get off until later. She went home and changed and then came back to Baja and sat there waiting for me to be done. People just kept coming in and I kept thinking I would be done and then get stuck there for another hour making drinks. The anticipation was building. Finally, it was around midnight that I was done. We were trying to think which bar on the street would be the one we'd least likely run into anyone who worked at Baja. We decided which one that was, and we went.

We sat at the far corner of the bar, and I believe we both had a beer and a shot. Then, we kind of just sat there. We both knew what was going to happen. We were about to kiss for the first time. My heart was pounding. We decided we should just go and get this over with, and we finished our drinks and closed out our tab. We walked outside and I was looking around for literally like a corner to hide somewhere so we could kiss. Abi, having lived near there before, said, "Why don't we go down to the beach?" I was like, you can just do that? You can just go walk on the beach at night? "Yeah, stupid." The exchange went something like that.

We walked down the beach a ways so that there were as few people around us as possible. I was so nervous. My heart is beating faster right now as I'm writing this. We finally stopped and I turned around to face her. My back was toward the ocean and a little downhill from her so I was at the perfect height to kiss her. I remember thinking the second before I went to kiss her that this was it. I was in love. And then we kissed and it was the most sensually, sexually, spiritually satisfying kiss I've ever experienced. Abi and I spent the next three to four hours walking up and down the beach, talking, kissing, holding hands. She got on a plane two hours later to Mexico. Let's just say I ruined that trip for her.

Dutch wouldn't meet Abi for 11 more days, my birthday. The first time Abi and I had sex was on my birthday, in my bedroom, in the house that I lived in with Donald and Owen. It was a shocker for Abi when she discovered *that* little detail. Fast-forward two weeks after that, and I'd asked Abi to drive up to Seattle with me and my friend who was moving back there and meet my family for Thanksgiving. Donald would obviously find out if Abi went home with me, so I decided to tell him a couple days before that Abi and I were dating. This was the straw that broke the back for my and Donald's relationship. I don't want to say too much more about Donald and I. There were times I think we mutually thought we could salvage the relationship, but it's never going to happen and I'm okay with that and I sure as hell hope he is too.

"Impressions in the sand while I hold your hand.

The sun peaking, our love sneaking.

I will never forget the feel of your hair, so short, so fair.

A love in me for you was born that day."

CHAPTER FOUR: A HOME IN TOPANGA

Abi and I had only been dating for two months when both of our leases were ending at the same time and we had to figure out what to do. I suggested to Abi that we move in together. It didn't seem weird to me. When I fall in love, I fall hard. I've lived with pretty much every girlfriend I've had since adulthood. Abi had been living with her brother for a number of years, and now she had to tell him she was going to be moving in with this guy she'd been dating for two months.

Looking back, I can see how reliant I was on having a companion next to me. Even if I didn't have an official "girlfriend," most nights I would have someone stay with me, and they were usually female. I've never really shown a significant amount of independence, but I certainly always felt as though I had. Abi was no different, but her personality is unlike anyone else I've ever known. I truly look up to her as a person.

Abi came with a small chihuahua, Baxter. (Mr. Baxter and Mister-Sister also became acceptable names for him.) This brought the number of dogs in the house to three, so we couldn't exactly move just anywhere. We looked at one apartment in Hollywood. It was okay, but there just wasn't enough room, and we wanted some place where we could let the dogs outside and not have to walk them every time. Thus enters someone who, even though he didn't know it at the time, would become an integral player in my life: Bruce.

Bruce was a regular at Baja Cantina. Abi had known him for a while, and they were good friends. Bruce would take the girls out to dinner or mani/pedis. Initially I swore that Bruce was gay, but he's been married to the same wonderful woman since age 18. He just grew up with all sisters and relates very well to women. Bruce grew up in Topanga, California, a small community in the canyons near Malibu. He recently had to put his mother who was living in their house up there into a nursing home. Bruce was at the bar explaining that he didn't know what to do with the property now, and maybe he'd have to start renting it out. Abi overheard this and raised her hand. "Uh, Ryan and I are looking for a place to move into!" Bruce tried talking her out of it, saying the house is built all weird and it's way far away, you won't like it, etc. Abi said she wanted to check it out anyway.

It was winter, so the sun was setting pretty early. Abi and I left from my house in Hollywood to go and see the Topanga house. It did seem like it took forever to get there. I mean, I wasn't even sure if this was Los Angeles anymore. The sun went down, and we were on Old Topanga Canyon Road, and there are no lights. The road weaves back, and forth and our GPS went out on our phones because there is no cell service up there. We knew the house was on this road—we just had to keep an eye out for the address. We eventually found it and finally made it up the driveway and parked.

The house was pitch black inside. We didn't know where to walk in from. We made it in and found some lights and sure as shit, the house is really strangely laid out. It was built in the 1920s and was used originally as a hunting cabin. From there someone expanded it in the 50s, then built a bunch more onto it in the 70s, and eventually I built a room onto it myself in the 2010s, so the house definitely has some history behind it. We walked around for a bit and looked at each other and said hell, why not? The house needed some major face-lifting done, but Abi likes that kind of stuff so I think she saw its potential. I just thought it would be amazing to live in a house with a big yard, and the deal Bruce was giving us on rent was too good to pass up. So we told Bruce we'd take it.

Abi and I began to settle into our new home with our new combined "family." Dutch was still very much a young dog, and I would take him with me on hikes around the canyon, exploring all of the different trails and paths. It was reminiscent of the house back in Everett, at least the feeling of being connected with nature again. As I've learned and become older, I've become much more conscious of my need to be close to nature. I felt it as a kid when I would play in the woods behind my house, and I feel it again now. If I ever live in New York, Central Park better be on my doorstep.

* * *

Ironically enough, Abi and I moving to Topanga coincided with the beginning and ultimately completion of my second feature film, *Evidence*. Before Abi and I moved in together, I was staying at her place in Venice. We were watching the first *Paranormal Activity* movie on DVD. It already had its run on the big screen, and I was very aware of the story of how the movie hit, why Paramount decided to pick it up, how much it was allegedly produced for, etc., but I wanted to see if it lived up to the hype. Spoiler alert, it didn't. Not for me, at least. But it did for millions of others, and that's what intrigued me.

Abi and I walked outside on her porch to smoke a cigarette. It was January and there was a heavy rain. I think it was the last year it rained like that in LA for the next six years or so. We sat there discussing the movie and where we thought the movie failed to deliver. They just didn't go big enough in my head. I had never considered doing a found-footage film like *Paranormal Activity* or *Blair Witch* before, but something in me said, "I can do that...only bigger." It was then and there that I decided to make a movie and Abi would be in it.

We began coming up with a story and where we could film it. We thought about who we could ask to come on board and help. What about Brett and Ashley? They worked at Baja with us and were both trying to gain careers as actors. Hey, Ashley's got some connections to some gear, maybe she could help? And just like that, we were off to the races. Here's where it's interesting and part of the reason I wanted to write this book; to go ack and think about periods of time in which I shifted gears and started getting shit done, vas I being manic? Either way, the movie never would have happened without me, manic r not. I don't want to come across as arrogant—those are just the facts. No one around us even still to this day) were trying to make a feature film. Short films, sure, but I didn't see he point in doing those. It was almost a total miracle how that film all came together in the nd and I was the engine that was driving the train.

I'm trying really hard to remember exactly how I did it, but I can't. Like I said, I hifted gears. The only thing that mattered to me was how the hell to I pull this all off. hree months later, we were rolling camera! A week goes by, and all of the sudden "RV Veek," as we called it, came up. I was dropping some serious cash now for things, but we're etting the shots! It's *working!* Everyone was working their butts off. It wasn't easy, and here was drama, but one of the greatest things about Abi's and my relationship is when we vork together, we operate differently. We are able to completely make that shift from ersonal to professional. Abi is also extremely smart and knows how to work people and alk them in the direction she wants. I am a natural-born leader who's boots on the ground nd leading the charge. I would be concentrating so hard on getting the job done, that Abi vould watch the drama that was going on and be able to work that stuff out so I didn't have o worry about it. The two of us make a hell of a good team.

But just like any other family, which is what we all had become, there are just as nany highs as there are lows. I know there's a picture somewhere with all of us and we're ll each holding up a dog and Dutch is there. I'll try and include it in this book. I talk pretty adly about *Evidence*, because I believe it to be cursed, and it's almost killed me twice more on that in a later chapter), so instead I'm now going to write about my three favorite noments while making *Evidence*.

* * *

If I did some digging on my laptop, I could probably figure out what the date was exactly of our first day of shooting, but I can tell you that we had three locations, two of hem both interior and exterior and the third a driving sequence, and we had to get it all hot and done before the sun started to go down in order to maintain consistency in ighting. Little to say, there was a lot of shit that had to get done, and I had to coordinate it ll, along with acting and filming most of it. I was on a bit of an edge. I had to wake up early nd pick up Howie, then fight traffic to Hollywood where we were going to shoot the pening scene at Brett's place.

From there, we met up with Zach, broke for lunch, then had to "steal" a shot on Iollywood Blvd. where Zack was dancing around on a street corner and there were cops atrolling around and we, of course, had zero permits. Meanwhile, I'm checking in with Abi and making sure she's got everything going at her brother's place, which was going to be the third and final location. I was worried they'd wear the wrong wardrobe or, worse yet, wouldn't show up on time and we wouldn't finish before sundown. My head was spinning.

We loaded up and headed to Santa Monica where Brandon (Abi's brother) lived at the time and we were able to not only get everything we needed, but it was perfectly timed to the end of the day. We had done it. More importantly, *I* had done it. I rode in the back of Brett's Jeep Wrangler back to his place to pick up my Jeep and drop Howie off before going home. The top was down, and Howie was sitting in the front seat with Brett. They were talking but I couldn't hear because of the wind. So instead I just sat back and looked around at my city and what I had just accomplished that day that a lot of people say they can do, but to actually do it is a feeling I will always enjoy.

The next story takes place at Howie's apartment, where I was editing the movie. We had filmed about 75% of it but still had no location for the ending and weren't sure about *how* to end it. I remember very vividly, I went out on Howie's porch to smoke a cigarette; it was later in the day. Howie and I were discussing the problem I just laid out. Howie said, "You know…Keith knows a guy who might be able to get us a helicopter for cheap." "How cheap?" "Like a thousand bucks…?" "Fuck me…" as I blew out toxic smoke, "I think I have to put a fucking helicopter in the movie now."

When I decide to do something, like something big or bold or something that could turn out terribly wrong but I decide to do it anyway, I reverse-engineer the problem. I don't see how everyone doesn't operate in the same way. It's that same "click" in my brain I've been talking about. Once I decide on something, it's like it's already happened in my mind; I just have to work backwards from there. It's very weird.

So now knowing how we would end the movie, I crafted a story (more like a series of actions to put our characters through in order to get them to appear in this open field, the only place we could get the helicopter to land) and set up to arrange the helicopter. We set a date and recruited as many of our friends as we could to get out there as extras. The day we picked just happened to be Ashley's birthday, and I always joked about how I gave her a $1,300 birthday present: a helicopter ride! Deep down I was hoping I could get a ride in it, but we only had a limited amount of time because of fuel, and I'm a producer first and wanted as many takes as we could get. I'll ride in a helicopter some other day.

We got tons of coverage. A fleet of Navy helicopters flew overhead, and we were able to cut some of that footage in as well—it was incredible. I remember saying goodbye to our pilots, who were super cool, by the way, and standing with my hands on my hips, watching the fucking helicopter I had just rented for the day for *my* movie fly away. It was a level of accomplishment nobody I knew of had even dreamed of attempting, and I clung onto the feeling it emitted so I would know what it feels like in the future. That feeling, for me, is the ace in my sleeve. I think I am addicted to that feeling and that's why I will outlast, outwork and outhustle every other person in my profession. Being clinically psychotic also helps.

My actual birthday is November 11, but this last story just happens to coincide with my 30th birthday *party*, which was Tuesday, November 9, 2010. There is a big film market held every year in Santa Monica during the first week or so of November called the American Film Market or AFM. It's where a ton of different sales agents, distributors, production companies, etc., get together and shop their films around. We had completed *Evidence* and I had prepared screeners, press kits, trailer, website, everything. My mission was to take our movie there and sell it. I spent the entire month prior making phone calls, sending emails, scheduling pitch meetings, everything. I was getting a lot of things booked because people liked that I already had a finished film and was not asking for funding. If you can afford to and it doesn't cost much, just go make a movie yourself and then sell it. As long as it feels like a complete movie, someone out there will buy it.

I bought the half-pass so my first day began on Saturday. I went nonstop from early in the morning to late in the evening, taking meetings, networking, bullshitting, constantly pitching myself, my movie—it's on a whole different level. Everyone there is so full of shit, it's tangible. It's also extremely exhausting. I would come home, refill my publicity materials, make notes on who I met with and try and keep that organized, double-check I had everything ready, pass out, wake up, and do it all over again the next day. I've learned from attending various film festivals and markets over the years that four days is just about my limit at one of these things. At least take a day or half-day off and then go back at it if you have to, but four days in a row of pitching is mind-melting.

I was aware that my birthday was coming up, but it wasn't until Thursday, the 11th. It was Tuesday, and I had just finished my last day at AFM—everyone else had too. My body and my brain were done. All I wanted to do was go home and pass out. But Abi's brother, Brandon, and his best friend, Corey, insisted on taking me out to a nice dinner in Santa Monica because they were going to be working on Thursday and wouldn't be able to come up for my actual birthday. I said honestly, gents, I'm so tired I can't. But they pushed and I finally said fine.

I was literally falling asleep at the table. I ate a fantastic meal and was looking forward to going home. But, Brandon and Corey wanted to go out for drinks—it was my 30th birthday coming up and they wanted me to rally. It took some convincing, but I finally decided to do it and we started ordering shots. We left the restaurant, and Brandon said he had to stop by some new bar on Main St. to drop off an application because he wanted to work there, and then we'd head down to O' Briens or someplace like that. I was still reading and replying to emails and text messages from AFM, so my head was buried in my phone as

I followed them into this bar. We walked downstairs, and my head is still down in my phone and I'm literally following Brandon's shoes to where he's going, not looking up at all. He leads me to the back and we walk into this room and I hear a crowd of people shout, "SURPRISE!! HAPPY BIRTHDAY!!!"

My jaw dropped and I looked up from my phone and looked around the room. It was everyone...EVERYONE I knew at the time from all different circles of my life. People who had never met each other, but each one was significant to me in their own way. Everyone was dressed in black and my eyes landed on a figure standing in the middle of it all, it was Abi. She looked so unbelievably gorgeous, sexy, tall, confident, glowing. She looked at me and smiled. I will never forget that look. She fucking did it, man. Words didn't need to be exchanged at how grateful and thankful I was. I don't think I'll ever top that one.

So when I think about *Evidence*, I usually think of all the shitty times. But it's what we gain from those experiences and choose to either let them define us or use them as an excuse for anything you don't have. Or, you can choose a different path, a higher path, and decide to instead continue to persevere. I chose the latter.

All of the amazing things that began to happen because of *Evidence* quickly faded away. The "family" we had built over the last two years was fading. I know my sales agent I signed with, Yarek, made money from my film. I didn't make a dime and still haven't. I have seen Yarek twice since then—once in passing at AFM, years later, and once about two weeks ago at a party my producing partner and I held. I'd be lying if I said my first instinct when I saw his face was to walk over and beat the living shit out of him, but I'll just ruin his life instead. Fuck him.

Nobody, especially Howie, the director, believed that there was no money. Howie truly thought I was sitting on top of this big pile of cash and was fucking everybody over. How wrong he was. I may subconsciously use people—I'm narcissist. But one thing I pride myself on is being loyal to a fault. Never in my life would I dream of fucking anybody over like that. And if Howie, or anyone else who doubted me, was in my position and actually knew everything, they would have a different opinion. That's why it can be lonely if you're the last line of defense. When it all fails, you have no one else to blame or point your finger at. I'm proud of the movie, but I'm not ignorant of the fact that I fucked up the sales and distribution part of it, and that's my loss and *only* my loss, and I wear it well and in very much plain sight for everyone to see. My "Scarlett Letter," if you will. Ironically enough, the last memory I have of us all being together coincides with the first time I realized Dutch was mortal and is going to die.

* * *

We were having a party for some reason or another up at our house. The annoying thing about having people over is making sure the dogs don't get out. We have a big yard, but it's not totally fenced in, and we live next to a road where it's dark as shit at night and people like to drive really fast on it. As the night went on and we got drunker, we usually end up not worrying that much about making sure the gates stay closed. I hadn't seen the dogs in a while, but it's not like I noticed they were gone; I just assumed they were taken care of. Suddenly, I see Hauser and Dutch arrive by the back door, panting and out of breath. I knew they had gotten out and seeing how hard they were panting, I knew they'd been gone for a while.

I got pissed that people can't keep fucking gates closed (to this day, I don't get it) and checked the dogs to see if they were okay. Hauser has tan fur and I could see he was dirty, but no cuts or anything. Then I noticed Dutch was acting weird. He has black fur and he always looked a little dirty, so I held him in my lap. That's when I noticed he was covered in oil. I looked closer and he had several cuts up his leg and side. He'd been run over by a fucking car. I lost it.

I fucking yelled at everyone to get the fuck out of my house right now. I don't even think it was 9 o'clock yet, but I didn't care. I shut that party down hard. Because I was feeling something I never felt before with Dutch. He could have *died*. My head went straight to, holy shit, what if Dutch was gone? He can't leave me, not yet. I washed Dutch and in the shower I cried and told him how much I loved him and how sorry I was that I had let this happen. He ended up being fine, the tough son of a bitch, but I knew in my head that I only had a little longer with Dutch. This was a sign, I just knew it.

"We see signs in life, telling us everything and anything is possible.

It's easy to hear and see the good ones; it takes a different level of self-reality to be able to identify the bad signs, and instead of burying them within ourselves, we must let them encourage our actions."

CHAPTER FIVE: TIME

I was so certain that *Evidence* was going to be the key my having finally "made it." A little bit of advice: If you live thinking that the term "made it" in the entertainment industry is a real thing, then get the fuck out of my industry. There is no "made it." If it's all you can possibly think of doing for the rest of your life, then you have already "made it." Got it? That's not something you can decide on your own.

I had quit working at Baja and was basically waiting for the money to come flowing in from *Evidence*. Little did I know there wouldn't be any money coming. I began looking around for any work I could get. Years before, I would do work around my dad's house and he'd pay me $12 to $15 an hour or so. I didn't mind the work—at the time it was a lot of landscaping and building retaining walls. A water pipe had burst and flooded the house while he was out of town on a trip, but he ended up using that as an excuse to give the house a much-needed remodel. Now the house was about 80% gutted, and my dad wanted to rebuild it all himself. He knew I needed money, and so he offered for me to come up to Everett for a few weeks at a time and I could work on the house, make some money, and spend time with him—seemed like a win. It's hard to see from the inside, but looking back on it, I was definitely going through a manic phase at the time and I want to go back and talk about that two- to three-month period of my life before I got married.

I was going to write some background on my relationship with my dad, but I'm starting to think that it really doesn't matter. Just like any other parent, he did the best he could, which turned out to be not very well. My mom was adopted at birth, so I have no idea what health traits/problems I inherited on my mom's side, but I do know that my dad's dad suffered from bipolar disorder as well. He had been dead for a number of years before I was told this. In fact, I didn't find out my grandfather had been bipolar until months after I was diagnosed. I finally built the courage up to tell my dad about my breakdown and diagnosis over the phone and the first words out of his mouth were, "Why didn't you call me so I could come down there?" Followed by, "You know your grandfather was bipolar too." Nope, didn't know that, Dad. Thanks for the information.

But during the time I worked on the house, my father and I were getting along okay. I was really amped and excited to remodel the house. He walked me through and explained to me everything he was going to do. I was excited because I still loved that house and it deserved a facelift. I was *convinced* I was going to get everything done in the next month or so and my dad could finally relax in a beautifully finished home. I was going to work 10 to 12 hours a day and then stay at Shane's house. Shane and his then-fiancée were getting married, and I was going to officiate and then house-sit for them while they went on their honeymoon; I was really excited for this plan.

My dad does nothing without extensive research, planning, and eventually near-perfect execution. I work in a very different and faster manner than him. This caused friction for several reasons. The first time I can remember thinking, my dad's crazy, he'll never finish this house, was when I had built the entire framing and ran electrical through all of it on a stretch of the downstairs wall. It was probably 20, 25 feet in length. I was super proud of it. My dad was out of town for a few days, but he trusted me to work on things when he was gone. When he got home, I showed him what I had accomplished. He was impressed until he started measuring. The wall leaned out by less than half an inch. That half an inch was enough for him to tell me we'd need to tear it down and do it again. It had taken me two days—alone—to complete this wall. Tearing it down and doing again at *his* pace would take a week. I kept my cool and said all right, Dad, I'll tear it all down.

During this time, Abi and I would constantly be either talking to each other on the phone or FaceTiming. We literally went from never being apart for a single day since we first kissed to now being apart for weeks at a time. When I tell you I need to be around that woman, I *need* to be around her. She literally charges my battery when I'm around her, even if we're just sitting there, and I know I do the same for her. It's very weird, really. Anyway, we were apart now, and it was weeks at a time. My dad would fly her up for a few days to see me a couple times, but we were going mad. Let me tell you how this eventually led to us getting married.

On one such trip up, my dad also used his hotel points so we could spend a night downtown in Seattle. I surprised Abi with it. I remember me driving around Seattle, trying to remember where exactly this hotel was, and Abi kept asking me if I knew where the hell I was going and why I kept having to turn around. She was happy and surprised when I told her what we were doing. If you've never been, Seattle's a pretty cool city to hang out for a night or two, at least I like it. It's small enough, and if you don't mind walking, you can get around to pretty much every area of the downtown/Pike Place area. The Art Institute of Seattle is near there, so I knew the area pretty darn well. Shane and his wife were meeting us for drinks. There's one thing to note about Abi and I, when we vacation, we vacation hard and usually drink our faces off. We had a reservation at a really fancy but cool restaurant. We started doing shots and then next thing I know Abi is running down the street because she wants to put her feet in the water and I'm screaming after her. We then crawled—yes, crawled—up the sidewalk pretending we were climbing a mountain or something like that and made it to the restaurant just in time. This was all while it was still daylight and there were people everywhere staring at us.

Before we met Shane for drinks, Abi and I were shopping at a mall downtown. Already having a strong buzz from the free shots we just got at a bar because I still knew the GM, we wandered into kind of like a Hot Topic store. There was this spindle thing on the counter by the register that had all these rings and earrings for like 5 to 15 bucks. Abi and I found a simple silver ring with vampire teeth on them, and something inside both of us decided right then and there that we should get married. Like, today.

It was past four o'clock so we said that we'd go down to the courthouse in the morning and get married and this would be her wedding ring. Maybe that's a reason we got so shit-faced is we were secretly celebrating us getting married. That night, we picked up an 18-pack of Icehouse and a bag full of those supplements they sell at the counter to supposedly enhance sex and stumbled back to our hotel. We both woke up the next morning with a hangover. Not from the booze necessarily, but from our decision to get married. Neither one of us said anything about it for probably the first two or three hours of the day, where we just laid in bed watching network television, but finally one of us brought it up and we both agreed that we were crazy. We can't get married just like that, it's nuts. We laughed it off and went and saw *Transformers 3* in IMAX.

* * *

Abi went back to LA, and I continued working at my dad's house. I remember where I was when a real conversation of when Abi and I would get married happened. I was out front of my dad's house, walking up and down the sidewalk because I got shitty reception inside. I'm pretty sure she's the one who suggested it, but my birthday was coming up and it was going to be my 11/11/11 birthday. My entire life, I always knew that date was going to be important in my life. I used to think, that's the birthday where I'll be a huge baller and throw this epic rager that goes down in history. Much better than that, it was going to be the day I married my soulmate.

The plan was, we would tell nobody, but we'd make an open invitation to my friends/family and Abi's friends/family, that we would be celebrating my birthday in Vegas for 11/11/11 and then she and I would sneak off for a few hours, get hitched, then party our faces off and surprise everybody. We both were caught off-guard a bit once we decided on a plan, because we couldn't believe we were actually going to get married. I had ZERO excitement about working on my dad's house anymore, and I wanted to be back in LA with Abi more than anything.

Remember before when I said I was most likely acting manic during this time? Well, it eventually came to a head with my dad and ended up blowing into a huge fight and me giving up on trying to fix his house. I'm going to tell you what happened as best as I can remember.

The possibility of me fixing his house, and when I say fix, I mean he was only eating meals he could prepare in a microwave in the laundry room. There was framing still to be done, electrical, water pipes to be installed, there was no carpet or floor of any kind—there still isn't, by the way— but it was impossible because like the wall story I told you before, for every step or two of progress I'd make, he'd decide he wanted something different, or his attention would focus on a *different* project and then he'd get all crazy about that one. I was working my tail off, but I would look around and say, it's hopeless. I *pleaded* for him to hire someone to help, a professional, but he didn't trust—doesn't trust—anyone. It's a weakness in him that is only getting worse with his age. I haven't been back to that house in almost four years, and I'm not sure if it will ever fully get finished. And maybe that's okay. Restoring that house has become almost like his white whale. He lives to work on that house. If he finally finished it, I don't think he'd be very happy because he wouldn't have anything to chase after anymore.

I was frustrated, plus I missed Abi even more immensely now that we had decided to get married. I was venting my frustrations onto my dad and the house, telling him he needs to switch his mind or else he's never going to finish. He just couldn't believe what I was saying. He didn't know why I was getting so upset. I can't remember what exactly it was, but I lost my shit on him. I was crying and screaming at the same time. I hate this, but it's the truth. Something about my father's reactions to things and inaction on so many others causes me a lot of anger. As I was screaming at him, he kept telling me I'm being bipolar—I'm being bipolar, I thought, why are you so bipolar? Like probably 98% of other people, when I heard the term bipolar, I thought split personality. I remember thinking, I'm not bipolar, I'm just fucking ANGRY. Everyone has a temper when pushed far enough.

We were standing at the top of the stairs yelling. Years before, before I met Dutch, I remember standing at the exact same spot feeling the same type of anger, yelling and screaming at my dad and walking out to go and live with my sister. Guess who the first person I called was after I stormed out this time: my sister.

I called her crying and asked if she would come pick me up. I'd already started walking toward her house. I had been venting my frustration with my dad and that house for a while, so she knew I was hurting. My sister's been there for me at some crucial points in my life. We don't talk as much anymore, but thinking back, even to when I was a kid, she's been there for me. There was one time I remember riding my bike through my neighborhood. Some older kids started following me and ran me off the sidewalk and I subsequently fell off my bike. My sister just happened to be in her friend's car, driving past and saw me on the ground and the kids walking toward me. She got out of the car and went off on those kids. I've never seen my sister be such a fucking badass as I did that day. It's interesting, because my sister doesn't remember this event, yet it stuck in my head. It just goes to show, you never know what you say or do to another person, good or bad, how those can have a life-long effect on that person.

Needless to say, I never worked on that house again. I was supposed to stay another two weeks, but I told my dad we couldn't work on that house anymore together and asked him to move my ticket up to leave as early as possible. Two days later, I was leaving Everett for good and headed back to my home in LA. This is the last I want to talk about my father.

* * *

Abi and I had a time set for November 10, 2011, at around 11:15 pm to be married at the Heavenly Bliss Wedding Chapel in Las Vegas, Nevada. They were going to write in 11/11 as the date, even though it technically wouldn't have been. Abi and I have been on about five or six vacations together, our wedding included. She has managed to get food poisoning for about half of them. This was no exception.

Abi started throwing up every 30 minutes, so I called the chapel and asked if they could move it, which they did, to the next day, which would actually be on 11/11. Weird. By the way, Abi's birthday is on November 22. For those of you bad at math, 11 + 11 = 22. Anyway, we changed plans. I mentioned before that we made an open invitation to friends and family, but I'm not sure I actually invited any of them to come out. Shane flew in, I'm pretty sure he had a hunch, and Owen came out with us on my side, and then Abi's dad, stepmom, and brother all made the trip as well. We were both bubbling with anticipation, and I was freaking out a bit. Abi's dad was staying down the hall from us, and here I am about to take his daughter and go marry her without ever really having too many talks with him beforehand and not "asking his permission" either. In between bouts of vomiting, Abi and I agreed we still didn't want anyone else there when we actually got married, but that I would tell her brother and her father that night.

So, I waited until BC (that's what I call Abi's dad) and Terri were going to bed, thankfully early, and asked BC if I could talk to him in our room for a sec. I remember my heart beating out of my chest with nerves as he followed me down the hallway and into our room. I think I poured him a drink or got him a beer and we sat at the table together. What I write next is about as close to accurate as can be in terms of what I said to him. Meanwhile, Abi is coming in and out of the bathroom while throwing up and smiling at her dad, nodding her head and giving a thumbs up. Here was my "pitch" to Abi's dad that night after I told him I was going to marry her the next day: "Look, I fucking drink, a lot. I smoke, I've been to prison, I'm a fucking piece of shit and I've done some horrible, horrible fucking things in my life, but I love your daughter more than anything in this world and I'll fucking DIE before I let anything bad happen to her. I promise you." He replied with how he wished he could be there when we get married, but that he couldn't think of having a better son-in-law than me. My relationship with BE has grown tremendously over the years and I love him very, very much.

Next was her brother. The four of us (me, Abi's brother Brandon, Shane, and Owen) all went out to party. Brandon had taken some ecstasy and was rolling hard. Owen hadn't eaten yet and was super drunk. Shane made it his mission to find Owen some food. We made it to a food court at like New York, New York or some fucking place. I was nervous again, but not nearly as nervous to tell Abi's brother because I'd already told her dad. I found a moment where Shane had taken Owen away to grab some pizza, and Brandon just came out of the bathroom. I told him that this whole Vegas birthday trip was a ruse and proceeded to tell him that I was going to marry his sister tomorrow. The very first words out of his mouth were ,"I'm going to have a brother?" We proceeded to have a long and loving hug and then we all went to the strip club and partied our asses off in secret celebration.

Abi had stopped throwing up, but was nowhere near 100% by the next day. In retrospect, food poisoning is a great way to quickly shed some pounds. She looks absolutely incredible in our wedding photos. I look like a chubby Sopranos wannabe. Anyway, we snuck off in the afternoon. We had some time to kill, so we had a few drinks and shots at the Stratosphere beforehand. It's a little nerve wracking when you start seeing a bunch of girls in wedding dresses running around having either just been married or about to be married. It was this constant reminder of "Are we really doing this?" I had always pictured being married, but we were both still freaking out a little bit.

Long story short, Abi and I were married outside, standing on green Astroturf, holding plastic flowers, while an Asian dude read generic wedding lines and one other guy standing off in the background held a boombox that played whatever wedding song they play when the bride walks down the aisle. It was perfect.

The ceremony lasted less than 10 minutes and we finished signing all the proper papers. The plan was we'd go back and surprise everyone—Abi would wear her wedding dress all night, and we'd party our faces off, and that's exactly what happened. I remember driving Abi back to our hotel. It was official, we were now husband and wife. I'm sure a lot of guys out there say this but I want to say it now. My level of commitment to Abi is beyond those of regular human capabilities. It's as certain as I know the sun will rise tomorrow. It's totally unexplainable, but over time the signs have become clearer and clearer that my soul was meant to find Abi's and we did. I believe there is one true soulmate out there for every single human on Earth. I don't know what the odds are, and it's impossible to measure because you ask any married couple, at least in the first few years, and they'll say their partner is their soulmate, but I just know it to be true. It's a fact in my eyes, not fantasy. I've also promised Abi that I'll die 20 or 30 years before her so that she can enjoy the last days of this life without having to deal with me. I couldn't imagine how difficult it must be being married to me. I have a hard time being married to myself sometimes.

* * *

Time passed. I began working at a different bar but on the same strip as Baja Cantina. This place was called Cabo Cantina and they run happy hour twice a day for four hours and it's 2-for-1 on drinks. Their policy is if a customer orders one beer, you pop them two, even if they don't want it. If someone orders a shot, they get two, or it's a double, even if they don't want it. It's a fucking shit-show. I'm going to tell you three stories that happened to me while working at Cabo. These, like everything else in here, are 100% true.

One night, I was working the bar downstairs. I was also a manager, so I could have security throw people out if need be and was basically in charge of keeping order around that place. A guy came up to my bar and he was not doing well. He was swaying and couldn't speak clearly. I told him he had to get the fuck out, now. His buddy came up, who seemed completely sober by the way, and said his friend just needed some water and that he had too much to drink. I told him it wouldn't matter if he drank some water and that he needs to get him the fuck out of my bar. Just as I finished saying that, the drunk guy threw up all over my bar. The puke ran over the back of the counter and spilled onto the plastic cups and blenders we used to make drinks. I lost my shit. Security came up and hauled the dude outside and our poor busboy had to clean it up. I then turned to the guy's buddy and told him to get the fuck out of my bar too. He put his hands up and said, "Why? I'm not even drunk!" And I said, "I know, but you're too stupid not to listen to me, so I'm kicking you out for being a dumb piece of shit!" Security led him out as well.

Another time, I was working the day shift and should have left a half hour before, but the place was packed for a game or something, and the switch over from day manager to night took some time for everyone to get settled. It was another one of those days where every fucking idiot in Venice just happened to come into my bar. I was on edge. I ran upstairs to count my drawer and as I came back down, this dude is smoking a goddamn cigarette inside, right there on the stairs. I couldn't comprehend it and I said, "Are you fucking *smoking* in here, bro?" And he was all like, "Yeah, so…" I fucking dragged his ass downstairs and threw him out the front door in front of a bar full of customers and told security not to let that dude back in, ever. When the guy yelled out why, I said, "Because you're either too stupid to be in here because you don't know you can't smoke inside, or, you're a fucking asshole who did it on purpose." The dude came back with, "Oh, yeah? Which one are you?" Security held me back as I fucking shouted, "Which one do you THINK, mother fucker!!!" There was a group of girls sitting right next to me, and they said I couldn't talk to customers that way. I think I said something about telling them to fuck off and then I walked back inside.

This last story could have ended up a lot worse for me. Not only did I hate the customers I had to deal with on a daily basis, but I was drinking at work and was probably manic as well. When that combination hits just right, my fuse becomes basically zero. I don't want to sound machismo or tough, but when it comes to a physical confrontation, my brain clicks over and I can't control my actions. If that weren't enough, corporate thought it was a good idea to have beer pong tables in every restaurant/bar.....fucking idiots who don't give a shit about their employees' quality of life.

It was a fairly slow night. There were a group of people playing beer pong and getting adequately wasted. A pair of dudes walked up and wanted to play winner. I kept my eye out, because anytime you have a bunch of douche bags in one room, drunk and doing something even somewhat competitive, chests like to puff up. Well, an hour later, guess what, I was right. There was some confrontation between one of the dudes and some of the people that were playing beer pong before. Drunk bitches can only make situations like this worse. Anyway, chests puffed and a skirmish began to break out. My gut instinct is always to rush in first, not ask security to do it.

So, I tried to pull apart the two guys when the walk-up dude takes a swing in my direction. I lose my shit. I grabbed him by the throat...yes, the throat...and slammed him down on the concrete steps as hard as I could. I then squeezed his neck to the point of him not being able to breathe, while I was screaming in his face, "Who's tough NOW, mother fucker! You fucking tough?! Come on, mother fucker!" I would let go of his jugular so he could take a breath and try and say he was sorry, but every time he began to speak, I'd squeeze his throat again, cutting off his air. Meanwhile, security was clearing out the rest of the other group but I just kept smashing his face into the ground and squeezing. One of the security guards, whose name I'm blanking on right now, but he was my boy, came up and was like, "Yo, Ryan...it's cool, they're gone. You can let him go." The rage subsided and I let up. I told security to walk him out, but out the back door.

I got up and looked around and saw fear in everyone's eyes. From customers, male and female, to the cocktail waitresses who worked there, and I was technically their boss during their shift. I'm tall, but not big or muscular, so maybe people assume I don't or can't fight. There was no question after that night, and word spread up and down the street, RYAN'S FUCKING CRAZY. Everyone up and down the block heard about what I had done. It actually earned me quite a bit of street cred and respect from the locals. It also gave the waitresses I was working with a sense of comfort. They knew I didn't fuck around and I would always watch out for them. I'm very fortunate that no charges were placed. I was completely over the top, but if you ask anybody who's ever worked at Cabo Venice, they'll tell you they would completely understand.

Now the reason I'm telling you these stories, particularly the last one, is because that is not normal behavior. This is the point of this whole book, to look back at moments and times where when they happened, I just assumed it was my anger or that I was just in my actions. Now, as a medicated individual, I can see that it was the illness coming out in me. It sounds fucking tough and everything to know the whole block was saying I was "crazy." And it's true, the girls *did* feel a sense of comfort when I was running a shift, but they also, at least some of them, were afraid of me. I'm not afraid of anything or anyone, not anymore. But I try and put myself in others' perspective and what that must feel like, especially to a female, that they are generally *scared* of you. I don't like that I have the ability to make people afraid of me. I'm not proud of it in the least. It's not fun, it's not cool, it's actually kind of sad for me. I'd much rather be known as a person who makes others happy, not a person who instills fear in someone else. The fear that at any moment I could fly off the hinges again, even if the intent of my actions are just.

Oh, well. Moving on.

During this time, I had a manager for my writing and film career that I would call regularly and bitch to him that I was done working in bars and I needed him to do *something* so I could quit. Whether that be money for a film, script, anything, I didn't care. Abi and I even changed his name on our phone at home to say "Better Be a Job" anytime he called, but he never delivered. Also during this time, something began developing with Dutch that would ultimately lead to his demise. A growth, very common for his breed/age/size, began growing on his back leg.

I have this thing that I don't like about me but I know exists, and that's not wanting to talk about things. For example, anytime the issue of me taking my medication comes up, I shut down. Anytime something comes up about my personal health and how I should go see a doctor, I shut down. And every time someone would ask me about Dutch's leg, I shut down. I have this knack for turning a blind eye to things. It's completely irresponsible. There's probably a dozen things I could fix on myself that I don't because I hate dealing with stuff. I suppose the closest feeling I could relate it to is being embarrassed? I don't know. My point is, a growth began to grow on Dutch's leg and I did nothing to stop it. It began to affect my interaction with Dutch. This thing was pretty gross, and I stopped petting him as much. I stopped cuddling with him. I rarely bathed him. We would keep him and Hauser gated off by the front door and not let them wander the house. I just didn't want to think about it because when I did, it made me extremely sad. It's not that I thought Dutch would live forever, it's that he had been the only thing there for me who got to see everything about me, and I was afraid to lose that. I now have a very different outlook on life and death. I encourage death more and understand the beauty that the gift of life is. We are all stardust, baby.

"I hide the pain anytime it's real.

I push it aside so I don't have to feel.

Not healthy,

Not smart.

But those are the cards I always deal."

CHAPTER SIX: LIFE AND DEATH

You know how parents always say the day my child was born was the best day of my life? Well, I'm not sure if they truly mean that or if they just feel like they have to say it, but the day my child was born definitely wasn't the best. Scariest day of my life, maybe, but not the best. Don't get me wrong—my son is one of the coolest human beings I could possibly ever care about, but the overall experience was exhausting. Even the final days leading up to it were filled with family intervening and complicating everything.

I won't go into great detail about the birth of Canon—that shouldn't be my full story to tell—but I'll do what I've been doing a lot of in this book and just tell you a few stories that happened during the pregnancy and subsequently Canon's birth.

A friend of Abi's, who became a friend of mine over the years as well, Kimi, was moving from LA to New York. She's a teacher who focuses on urban and low-income schools. She is one of the most genuinely good human beings on the planet. That, and she's a hoot to be with. It was summer, and Kimi was going to come up and stay at our house for a night and then she and Abi were going to have a Lifetime Movie Marathon the next day. So Kimi came up and we decided to go see a movie. *Pacific Rim* had just opened and so the three of us got ready and went to the theater.

We were all three just clicking and truly enjoying each other's company. Abi and Kimi call each other their sister-wives, and I soon became Kimi's sister-husband. If you've never seen *Pacific Rim* (2013) before, you absolutely must. It has one of the biggest and best openings in movie history in my opinion. It is 18 minutes long before the opening title appears, and the amount of setup, action, and reveal that is done in that opening is remarkable. Needless to say, the three of us were literally blown away by the experience. Notice I used the word "experience." I have a strong theory that who you see a movie with can either amplify or de-amplify your opinion of the movie. If you see it with a great crowd or group of people like I did, it heightens my enjoyment. Conversely, if you see a movie and the one buddy in the group got too drunk before, or keeps saying shit during the movie, it could be Citizen fucking Kane and I'd think the movie was just okay.

The reason I bring up this story is because little did I know that Canon's little body had already begun forming in Abi's belly. He was maybe two weeks old. Abi hadn't even told me, but she knew she was pregnant. I didn't find this out until just recently. Now it all makes sense....there's a reason *Pacific Rim* is Canon's favorite movie of all time. Big monsters and big robots. It was pleasing for me to find that out. It means perhaps Canon was there for that experience as well.

* * *

Abi is originally from Denver, although she's lived in LA the majority of her life now. In fact, we just did the math on it a couple days ago, and the house Abi and I have lived in here in Topanga is the longest she's ever lived than anywhere else in her life. They did a lot of moving as a kid. I thought that was a pretty cool statistic. Anyway, her family wanted to throw her a birthday shower in Denver. So Abi and I packed up Dutch, Hauser, Baxter, and our newest member, Gilbert the pig. (Abi has always wanted a pig her whole life. I'm the only idiot that said she could. FYI, if you are reading this, do not get a pig unless you have the land and property for it. Even then, they're just such assholes and not very friendly.) We rented a car and drove out to Denver.

I've done plenty of road-tripping in my days, and there were times I thought for sure I'd run out of gas, but I never have. I've had to coast down the hill and into the gas station before, but never stranded with an empty tank. Well, I was driving and Abi sitting next to me, of course. She was about seven months pregnant, so she had quite the belly on her. I had looked at the gas gauge a little while ago and it was just above a quarter of a tank. I figured we could push it a little longer before stopping to get gas. What I *didn't* know was that we were just entering the Rocky Mountains, and there are no gas stations, like for a while.

I casually brought up the fact to Abi that we need to stop for gas soon and she said what do you mean? What gas? She then saw how empty the tank was the mood dropped instantly. We quickly began to assess our options.

Option 1: Turn the car around and head back to where we knew civilization was.

Option 2: Keep driving and hope to God there's a gas station ahead of us.

I did the math in my head and realized that if we turned back now, I knew where the last gas station was that we passed and knew there was no way we would make it. So we pushed forward. The tension in that car was tangible. Neither one of us spoke a word. Suddenly, we see an exit with one of those blue and white signs of a gas pump and an arrow that pointed left. We decided to chance it. When we took the exit, we saw the arrow pointing left and it read gas in 22 miles. Abi said there's no fucking way we're making it another 22 miles, I said all we can do is try, and followed the arrows.

This road was in the middle of fucking nowhere. It was getting dark and there were no lights and no signs of anything. Abi and I started to run through different scenarios of what we would do if and when the car ran out of gas. My first thought was, I'll run ahead and Abi stays with the animals until I get back. Hmmm...a seven-month pregnant lady alone in a car by herself? No thanks. Okay, then...we both walk. And leave the animals in the car together? They'll murder each other. Oh, there's no cell reception either, by the way. You could hear a pin drop inside that car. Abi and I didn't have to say anything—we both knew he likely outcome that we were going to be fucking stuck out here and it would be 100% ny fault.

So, we just kept driving. All of the sudden, we came up and over a hill and there's a our-way stop sign with a post office on the right and a one-pump gas station on the left. hose were the only buildings in sight, I shit you not. My heart was racing because this hing looked like it hadn't been operated in 15 years. We pulled the car up and guess what, : worked! We filled that baby to the brim and headed back. The amount of relief I felt was ndescribable. Of course, on the way back to the freeway, I'm gloating to Abi about how I old her so and I've never run out of gas, blah, blah, blah. It cost us about an hour or so of ime added to the trip but in my opinion it was well worth it for the memories and the tory.

* * *

Now here we were, Monday, March 24, 2014. Canon's feet were positioned directly n Abi's back. I've never seen her in so much pain. The epidermal wasn't doing shit, it took terally an hour and a half to get an aspirin, and she was just miserable. Now here she is in abor for over an hour. Again, not my story to tell, but I'll tell you what was going through ny head. I was in there, I mean ALL IN where the action was happening. The doc was ointing stuff out to me and it's pretty incredible. He showed me the top of Canon's head, nd it looked so small. He was having a really difficult time coming out. Every time Abi ushed, I'd look and see if anything happened, and it was nothing. Like, no progress for an our. But, I kept telling her, "Oh, man! You're so close! It's about to pop out!" Meanwhile, 'm looking wide-eyed at the doc shaking my head thinking there's no fucking way this is oing to work!

The doc pulls out a suction cup and says he wants to suck him out by the head. I lidn't even know these things existed. Abi and I were like, uh….okay….whatever. He began ucking on Canon's head and I was not sure about it. On one contraction, he was pushing gainst the bed with one hand and pulling the suction cup on the other and suddenly it opped off his head. I looked at the doc and asked, "Is that supposed to happen?" "Oh, eah…all the time…don't worry," and he kept sucking.

Now, it was already past 11 pm. We were in between contractions and I looked up at he clock, it was about 11:03. I did the math and realized that she would be most likely aving a contraction right around 11:11. I said to myself, if this fucking kid is born exactly t 11:11, I'll flip. That contraction came and went and I said okay, whatever. Abi rested efore the next contraction and then that's when it happened. He finally came out. Time of irth was 11:18 pm. My thing about numbers will matter more in the coming chapters, but +1+1+8 = 11. Just FYI.

I didn't realize it but Canon was positioned face up, so when his head popped out, 1) I had no idea his head was going to be that big and 2) I had no idea that he would already look like such a person! He didn't look like a baby at all, he looked like a little boy to me. The first words Canon's ears heard after he left the comfort of Abi's belly were his father saying, "HO-LY SHIT!!!" The nurses put Canon on top of Abi's belly and she looked over at me in sheer panic. I was wide-eyed and shaking my head. We were both thinking, what the hell did we just *do?* They cleaned him up. I got to cut the umbilical cord, but I missed the placenta coming out because I was outside on the phone with my stupid brother. I didn't even know the placenta coming out was even a thing! Oh, well, next time I know not to leave before curtain call.

* * *

Now, I can only speak for myself, but once Abi and I had a child, the animals all took a back seat. Not sure if I've mentioned it yet or not, but I built a kennel and large structure for the boys. It was in the back yard and that was where Dutch and Hauser would stay anytime we left the house. During this time, the growth on Dutch's leg was becoming more prominent. It was no longer just a bump poking out of his fur; it was starting to look gross. It was embarrassing for me when people would comment about it and ask what it is and that I should have a vet look at it. I always brushed it off, saying I wasn't about to spend $1,000+ just to take a look. Then what? What if it were cancerous and they had to amputate Dutch's leg like they did my dad's dog, Barney? Not only did I not have the money, but I was not going to let Dutch go out like that. Something in me said Dutch would rather be dead than go out like a cripple. These were my own thoughts polluting my judgement.

The point is, I handled the growth on Dutch's leg like I handle most any other negative or uncomfortable thing I have to deal with in life, with that overbearing feeling of embarrassment. I'm very afraid to confront things of that nature. For example, I got a DUI several years back. Well, instead of owning up to my mistake and taking care of it right away by showing up in court, going to meetings, etc., I shoved the paperwork in a drawer and hid the mail from my wife. My license was obviously suspended, but I just didn't tell anybody about it.

But then, my license was about to expire. Nobody cares if your license is suspended if they check your ID at a bar, but they do care if it's expired. So, finally, with Abi's encouragement, I went to the courthouse to take care of it. I was there all day. They weren't calling my name. Finally, they did, and when the judge realized that I had been sitting on this DUI for five years, she was not happy and she sent me to jail for five days. I had to follow the bailiff out of the courtroom and go into a holding cell until they transported me downtown. I pleaded with the judge saying my wife was pregnant (which she was; this was before Canon was born) and if there was anything else I could do. She said nope. I asked if I could at least call my wife real quick from my cell phone, which she allowed me to do.

I tried to go out the door of the courtroom for some privacy but she wouldn't let me. So I went into a corner of the courtroom and told Abi. I told her what to do in order to get work covered and told her I was going to jail. The judge yelled at me to hurry up, so I told Abi I loved her and I'd call her as soon as I got the chance and hung up. Abi can tell you exactly how *she* felt about it—all I'll say is that she went out for drinks with Bruce just to have someone to talk to. That's when Bruce found out Abi was pregnant.

I'll sum up my time in jail quickly, because I think it's an important part of my story to tell but not necessarily life defining. The judge doesn't know it, although she was pleased once I got out and made all of my appearances and did all the classes and finally got it all settled, but what she did by not letting me get out of it and have to deal with the consequences of my actions was the best thing that could have possibly happened to me.

First story, I'm riding in the bus on the way to Twin Towers Correctional Facility. I was overhearing all the dudes talking about how if you get put in a certain section of Twin Towers, you're fucked. I'm thinking okay, just observe and follow what everyone else is doing and don't cause any attention to yourself. We get there and pull underground and they line us all up in a holding room. There were about three or four other busloads that had just gotten off. Within the first few minutes of getting off the bus, some dude clobbers this other dude next to me in the face and knocks him out cold. Everyone cleared the area as the first dude yelled at him, something about not fucking touching him when they were riding on the bus or some shit like that. I kept my eyes open and my mouth shut.

Second story, it took a while for us to get processed; I think it was somewhere in the neighborhood of 12 hours. At one point, we were all sitting in this room, waiting to be checked out by a doctor. The place is packed, dudes lying on the floor, sitting on benches; I couldn't ever really get comfortable—I guess that's the point. Suddenly, this compact white dude sits down next to me like he knows me. He starts going right into a conversation, and I start looking around. Not only were me and him some of the only white dudes in there, but I noticed that the blacks didn't sit with the Latinos and vice versa. Holy shit, this guy is sitting next to me because I'm white. I started talking to the guy, and he was telling me about how he was just in here 10 days ago and now he's back in for a month and he just can't get his life back on track. I remember thinking to myself, if I had my own business, whatever it was, I could help this guy. He just needs some help steering his ship straight. He would be so thankful and appreciative. I almost offered my phone number so I could get him a job at Cabo and then realized, what am I thinking? My turn came next and I stood up. We bro-hugged and he looked at me and said don't worry. Jail's over capacity, I'd be out in a day. I said we'll see, but I saw the confidence in his face—he knew what he was talking about and that made me feel better.

Last story about jail. After the two days they finally opened the cell door and called my name. I'll never forget that feeling. I quickly stood up and went to the door. They told me to follow the yellow line and that'd lead me to where I needed to go. I was beaming inside as I walked through the hallways. It was a feeling of accomplishment. I had faced up to my fears; the worst possible scenario has happened, but here I was, on my way out now. I had made it through. It took hours to get processed out, but eventually there I was, sitting on the floor, waiting to get my belt, money, phone, and this dude next to me looks down at my shoes and says, "Hey...I like your shoes, man. They look cool like that." I looked down at my lace-less shoes and said, "Thanks, man, my girl just bought them for me. Maybe I'll keep rockin' em' like this," and we both smiled. You want to see a happy face? Look at the face of a person about to get out of jail. Whether they've been there one day or one year, when that metal door opens and you get dumped back out onto the streets and into the world, it's one of the best feelings in the world. As I raced to get home in time to give Abi a big kiss and hug before she had to go to work that night, I decided that I was going to use this moment as a springboard to me getting my shit together and stop being afraid of dealing with things.

* * *

Dutch's leg continued to get worse. Eventually the lump was the size of a softball. It became a joke around the house and I had my own fun with it, although it was gross for me to touch. But I knew he was getting old. Abi's mom made me feel better about my choice to not have it removed. They have had a bunch of lab-type dogs, and they're prone to these growths, she said, and yadda, yadda, yadda. I knew Dutch's time was coming to an end. I had him for over 10 years now, I figured he had a little bit more in him. He was still Dutch, to a tee. He'd give that little half-ruff/half-bark thing that was so fucking annoying anytime he wanted inside, outside, or food.

I lumped Dutch into the same category of annoyance as the rest of the dogs, but the truth is, he was still my boy. I'd still give him more treats and pieces of food than the others. I'd still kiss his face...there was one certain place on the side of his mouth on his gums. That's where he liked to be kissed most by me. There were nights the kid would be asleep and Abi would be at work and sometimes I'd cuddle up and spoon with Dutch like we used to. I'd whisper in his ear how much he meant to me and how thankful I was for everything he'd ever done for me. I tried to show him that no matter what, he was still my best friend. And then one morning, I woke up to Dutch's leg bleeding...bad. I had no idea what I would ultimately have to go through that day.

I was working at this Italian place in Calabasas that I fucking hated. I was getting ready to leave for work, when Abi noticed Dutch had chewed on the growth and ripped it open and there was blood everywhere. I scrambled to find a bandage and did a half-ass job of wrapping him up. I had to get to work and I told Abi that should be good. She asked what do we do and I said I don't know, I have to go to work.

Well, it was only a few hours before Abi started calling my phone and told me the bandage came off and Dutch won't stop chewing at it. Thank God for that woman at that moment because I, of course, wanted to hide and do nothing. She told me if I could come home, she'd found someone who would come up to the house and put Dutch down for us. I held it together just long enough to tell my boss what was going on and that I had to leave. I waited until another bartender was able to show up and I went home. The coming paragraphs of what I write next won't be easy for me. I've already been crying uncontrollably these last few, but here we go.

When I got home, Abi was kneeling next to Dutch out back. He was lying on the ground and I could tell he was done. God damn...I fucking embraced that face of his and held it close. There were no words needed, we never needed them. Oh, God...I felt like he was the only thing that ever understood me. I thought about all of the times, the nights, the cries, the fights, the violence, the fucking, the bullshit, the arrogance, the emptiness, the lies, the deceit, the fucking HATE that brews in my body that I fight to control and change every day...I thought about how Dutch was always, ALWAYS there for me, through it all. He had my fucking back and I had his.

He would get up and pace around, panting heavily. Blood was dripping from his leg. We ended up on the hill next to some of the rose bushes, and he laid down on some grass that was now red with blood. I held him in my arms and laid there with him, telling him that he'd done a good job. He's fulfilled every single thing he was meant to fulfill. I told him how much I appreciated him and loved him. I heard a van coming up the driveway. It was time.

The guy who was there to put Dutch to sleep informed me of how it would go. He would give Dutch a shot first that would most likely make him throw up, and then he would give him a second injection that would put him down. I prepared myself. We laid Dutch on the dirt just outside my office window where I'm sitting now as I write this. The guy, who was so amazingly kind and courteous—this can't be an easy job for him—gave Dutch the first shot and sure enough, within a couple seconds, Dutch got up to throw up. I walked him around the corner and told him everything was okay. I encouraged him as he threw up and we walked back to where the guy was. He gave him the second shot and checked his pulse a few seconds later and said that he was gone. I said okay, and then I noticed something. Ants began crawling toward Dutch's body and wound especially. I brushed them away from his face and then looked at Dutch and realized this wasn't Dutch anymore; it was a piece of flesh, that if left there, would eventually be consumed and composed. My brain made a shift and I grabbed a shovel.

"Go out, chin up.

Go up, eyes wide.

My Brother-in—Arms,

You are gone but never

Forgotten."

ne of the first pictures Abi took with Dutch. We were about to go out for the night. I appreciate this one because it showed me Abi truly cared for him, even if Dutch doesn't represent it in this photo.

Hauser and Dutch during one of our camping trips up to the Kern River.

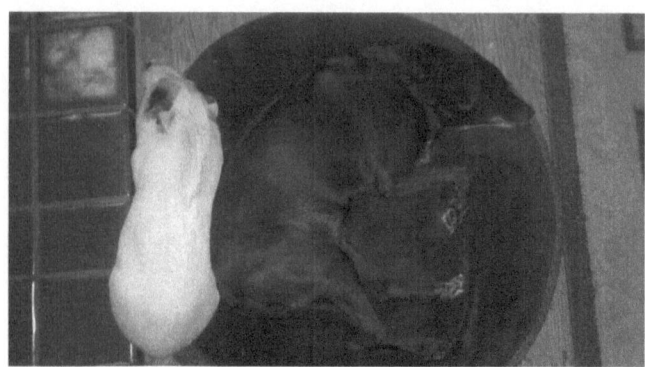

Dutch sleeping with Gilbert, our pig, early on in their relationship.

One of my favorite pictures of Dutch. This one was above the hill in the backyard of the house we lived at in the Hollywood Hills. I was living with Donald and Owen at the time.

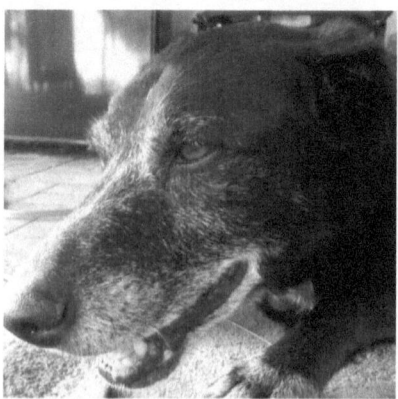

Dutch in his old age. You can see the grey in his face.

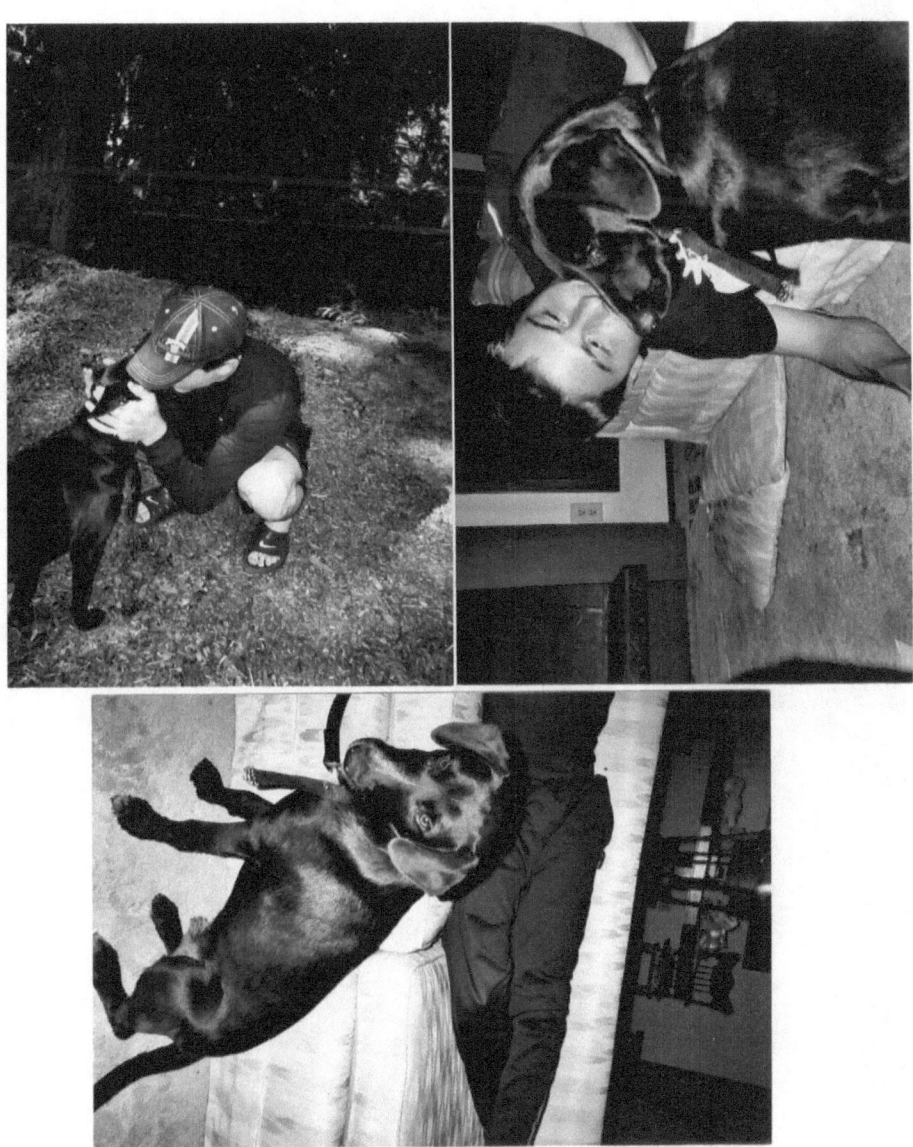

These pictures above are all from the first week I had Dutch.

Dutch enjoying a proper sleep on the rug of our house in Topanga. This was near the end.

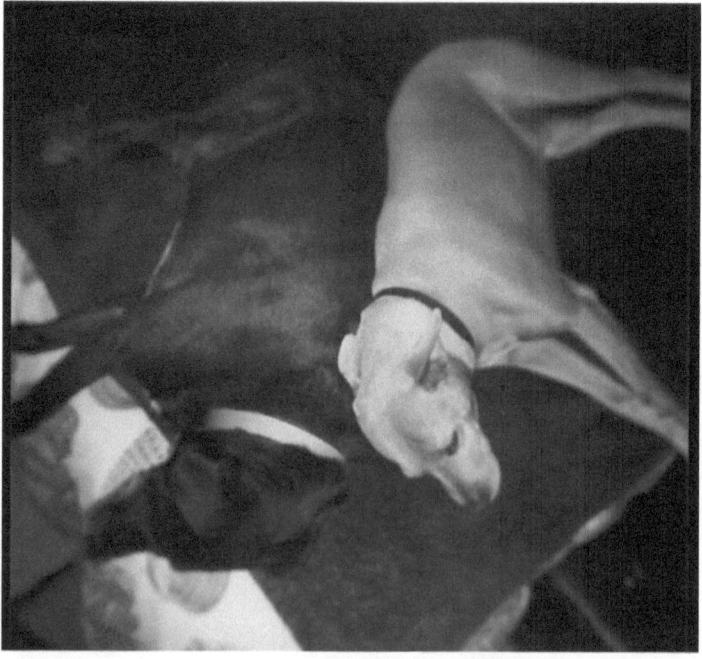

Dutch and Hauser having some nap time together. Hauser only knew of Dutch his whole life.

I will forever remember the look, feel and shape of his face.

This might be my favorite picture of Dutch. I'm grateful for Abi to recognize his importance in my life.

My mom, Charlotte, with Dutch as a young pup.

Dutch & Hauser spooning.

This picture is from the time I *almost* ran out of gas when Abi was pregnant.
Thanks for the memories, Dutch.

CHAPTER SEVEN: REMEMBRANCE

I dug a hole in the backyard under some trees. I guess it could have been deeper, but it was going to do the job. I covered Dutch in some plastic bags and wrapped him in a white towel. I laid my head on his body and sat there with him for probably 20 or so minutes before I laid him in the ground. I proceeded to fill in the hole. Canon wanted to help. I then searched around for some rocks and stacked them on top of the dirt. I found one smooth rock and I wrote something on it in black sharpie that has since faded away. All I know is that it had the words "Best Friends" on it.

And just like that, he was gone. Honestly, I just felt kind of numb about it. I thought previously about how I would deal with Dutch dying and how I didn't think there was any way I could get through it, but it seemed to happen so quickly that before I knew it, my years were gone. I'm actually very proud of how I handled the situation. For those of you who don't know, I have this weird thing with dead animals. Abi is the one who has to kill and get rid of any rats or mice that come into the house, and she also had to dispose of Hatty (a chicken) after a dog got into our yard and killed her. I don't have the same fear with dead people; in fact, I know it would be easier for me to kill a person over killing an animal. It's strange and hard to explain. That being said, I didn't hesitate even once to pick up Dutch's body and carry him to the back and bury him. I remember saying to myself as I walked him back there, "Ryan, you're holding a dead animal right now that should be freaking you out, but you're not." I could tell my brain had built up a wall to give me the strength to do it. This was one situation that Abi definitely didn't and couldn't handle. For some reason, she lost it.

I was also proud of how Dutch went out. It sounds weird, but I don't know, I've seen other dogs when they go and it's not always pretty. Dutch could have seized and had diarrhea all over the place. Nope, he took it like a champ. I was proud of him. That dog was one lucky and tough son of a bitch. He used to get out all the time. I can only imagine what adventures Dutch had when I wasn't around.

Over the coming days, I would wander back there to Dutch's grave, sometimes alone, sometimes Canon and I would go back there. I did a shitty job of putting the rocks up, plus I think some gofers or ground squirrels were getting in there because some of the rocks would always be pushed to the side from underneath. I would replace the rocks and put some more on top of it, but even to this day it's hard to tell *exactly* where he's buried. That's not the point, though. The point is that it comforted me immensely knowing that I still had my friend close by. It didn't feel like he was totally gone. It still doesn't feel like it, but I'll get more into that later.

* * *

Life moved on, and Dutch became just another memory. We moved the pig out in the kennel and out of the house permanently. He couldn't be happier because now he just got to go out and graze the entire property all day, plus we put a heated blanket in there and it's fully insulated. It's a *beast* of an animal house if I do say so myself. We noticed an interesting dynamic started to happen with the other animals. With Dutch out of the picture, there was no clear alpha anymore, and Hauser and Gilbert started fighting a lot and going after each other. Baxter and Hauser were fighting too; it took the two of them a couple of years before they figured out their status quo. I just remembered the first and only time Dutch established his dominance over Baxter. Let me tell you a story real quick.

Abi and I had only been living together for maybe a few months. Abi was meeting with Ashley and Howie at the house as we were prepping for *Evidence* then. I was at work (I swear, anytime Dutch did something like this, I was never there) and Baxter was sitting in Howie's lap, I think. Well, in typical Dutch fashion, for no reason and with no provocation at all, at least to a human eye, walked over and grabbed Baxter in his mouth and wouldn't let go. Baxter was freaking out, yelling. Howie was trying to get Dutch to let him go, but he wouldn't. Abi and Ashley were both rightfully freaking out. Eventually they got Dutch to let go, but ever since that day, Baxter bowed down to Dutch.

I went back work at the Italian place, but I was becoming increasingly more and more annoyed there. Let me explain. I have something that I find amazing some people don't have, which is something called *work ethic*. Abi has it too. What I mean by that is that if I'm employed by someone, even if I think that someone is a complete idiot and has no idea what they're doing, I still follow the guidelines and care about the customer's needs and wants first. I had been working in restaurants for over a decade, in all capacities and at all levels of management. Basically, I know what the fuck I'm talking about when it comes to the bar/restaurant business. It all came to a head one night.

We were getting slammed, and they put a girl behind the bar with me who had never bartended before. She was a cocktailer who convinced the morons in charge that she could do it. Well, spoiler alert, she fucking sucked. There were already two of us back there, plus the bar-back. This chick was getting in my way, not knowing how to make any of the drinks. I would have been much better off with just myself and the bar-back. My bar-back at the time was seriously one of the best I'd ever worked with.

Customers were complaining because all of their drinks were wrong, servers were bitching about missing tickets, I was pissed. One of the managers was standing at the host stand with his thumb up his ass, having no idea what was going on. They cared more about the dining room and chatting it up with customers than the actual production of service, especially in the bar area. I waited until there were no customers by him and I walked over and basically told him that he was a fucking idiot for putting this girl behind the bar with me, she's fucking up orders and customers are complaining. I told him he should do his job and pay attention to what's going on and then turned around and went back to my bar. Ten minutes later, I get called back in the office and they told me to go home, I'm suspended, and that we'd talk next Tuesday at noon. I knew right then and there what they were going to do. I said cool and walked out.

Well, Tuesday came and I went in and met with everyone. They sat me down in the office and pussy-footed around for 30 minutes before telling me they had my last paycheck and that they were going to part ways with me. I asked them why they didn't just lead with that instead of wasting my time. They handed me my last check, and I said great, where's my tips? It then took them another 20 or so minutes to figure that all out. I sat patiently in the office while they all scrambled around. "You sure you didn't pick them up already?" "Yep." It was truly the most awkward firing ever. I'm shocked at the amount of people who are in a supervisor or management position who are terrible at firing people. I fucking love it. I could make a living off of travelling around to different businesses and firing people. I don't give a fuck. This probably has a lot to do with my inability at feeling empathy toward others. I'm completely unemotional when it comes to that shit. I can see how it could be an asset of sorts in business, but as a human, it makes for a not very good life.

I said goodbye to some of the regulars who were sitting at the bar on my way out and I've never gone back in since. This was a milestone for me. I had been fired from a bartending job. This was hilarious. I went out the next day and was hired on the spot at this new Mexican joint, but it was more to prove to myself and to Abi that I could literally go walk the streets with a handful of resumes and come back with a job. I had done it at the Italian joint, and then I did it again at this Mexican place. But I didn't fit. I was done with the bar industry, or at least becoming very close.

* * *

The year was nearing an end. For my birthday, Abi and I went to have dinner at Monty's steakhouse. Very cool, old school Hollywood vibe (even though it's in Woodland Hills) with a piano man in the lounge. She had two presents wrapped for me. She had me unwrap one before we left. It was a squatty potty, which I must say I happily use daily. The other present was for me to open at dinner.

We got settled at our table and ordered drinks. Abi pulled out the gift and told me to open it. Little did Abi know, but I had gone up to Dutch's grave earlier that day by myself and talked with him. I wasn't in the best headspace at the time and was asking for some help, guidance, and direction, so I was already a little emotional that day. Plus, it's a birthday. I don't know anyone under the age of 35 who likes their actual birthday.

I opened the present and knew immediately what it was and I started to bawl. Abi had had this plaque made out of rock in honor of Dutch. It says MY BEST FRIEND, DUTCH and the date of his death which is July 25, 2015. I struggled through reading the inscription. The waitress came up at one point and I cry-laughed her off, saying I'm just a bit emotional, sorry! Abi put her hand on me as I got through it. Her intention was that Dutch could now have a proper tombstone, but I know Dutch. He wouldn't give a fuck about that, and I wasn't going to just leave it there if we ever moved. So, the "tombstone" now hangs on the wall in my office. This is what it reads:

God saw you getting tired
A cure was not to be,
So He put his arms around you
And whispered, "Come with Me."

With tearful eyes we watched you
And saw you fade away,

Although we loved you dearly
We could not make you stay.

A golden heart stopped beating
Your tender paws at rest,
God took you home to prove to us
He only takes the best.

I don't think I've read this whole thing since the first time I got it, and typing it out here, it comes off as cheesy, especially because Abi doesn't use the term "God" and neither do I anymore, but that's not the point. I did not see it coming whatsoever. It obviously hit me at a weird time that Abi had no idea about, but also the fact that Abi recognized how important Dutch was to me meant a helluva lot. This also told me that she loved Dutch too, even despite all his annoyances.

A couple weeks after my birthday, it was Thanksgiving. I love to cook on Thanksgiving, and because we have more room at our house than most others we know who live in LA, we usually have it at our place. We invite friends, family, we're pretty open about it. Dinner went great, drinks abound. Then, we were all standing around the living room venting our frustrations about how hard, hell, it's nearly *impossible*, to get a movie made. My friend Josh was there, as was Abi, when a thought came to me. Why not just do it ourselves? Invest in the gear, start a production company, and start making movies. Josh said he had the money to invest, he could get a line of credit through the SAG/AFTRA bank; we just needed someone who knew the technical side of things, camera, lenses, an editing computer, etc. I said, "What about Daniel?"

Daniel had been my DP on *Evidence*. I hadn't talked to him in two years. It was only about 10:30 pm so I went outside and called Daniel up. We quickly played catch-up and then I told him Josh and I were starting a production company and we wanted Daniel to be the third member. He said the timing was actually perfect because he had just finished doing camera work for a TV show and he had nothing coming up. We arranged to meet in a few days, and with that, RynoRyder/Boyer Productions was formed.

We came out, guns blazing, the following year. A week before Sundance was going on, I had the crazy idea that Josh and I should drive out there. The reason was, if we wanted to play with the big boys, we had to go where the big boys were. I remember walking outside and calling Josh and him saying, "Yeah, let's do it." He booked a place, and we scrambled to put together business cards that had a web address on it, but there was no website. Daniel was *literally* building the website while Josh and I were on the road driving out to Park City.

That first year at Sundance was truly a blast. I was straight up hustling the whole time. We had no idea what we were getting into or what to plan for. We didn't know where to go or what to do. We drove straight into downtown, not stopping at our hotel before, and hit Main Street. We found a bar, sat down, ordered a couple of beers and a couple of shots of whisky and toasted to our first year at Sundance. Ironically enough, the first person we sat down next to and introduced ourselves to, we would nearly become executive producers on a film of his two years down the road, although it eventually didn't pan out. My point is, say hello to everyone, and always stay in contact.

So for the next few days and nights, Josh and I handed money to door guys and chatted it up with bartenders, with anyone we could so we could get the in on where to be. We didn't *technically* get anything out of Sundance that year except the experience and knowledge. When we got back, I had already lined up our first "paying" gig: shooting a video for my friend, Devin. We were taking meetings with people I found through networking online, we ordered all the gear, Josh took out a loan, we went all in. That first year was a huge success; the next year, not so much. Since I'm about to go somewhere pretty dark in the next chapter, I'll sum up that first year on a positive note and tell you three stories from that year that I look back on with great joy and pride.

* * *

We had already done our first two shorts, *Apocalypse: The Hooker* and *Apocalypse: The Drunk* both of which are prequel stories of characters I'd written from a feature-length screenplay. We were tossing around ideas for which character to do next when my brother called. He told me his business partner's daughter wanted to get into acting, and if I could write a story set in this same *Apocalypse* world as the first two and include her as one of the characters, they were willing to put $4,000 to $5,000 into this thing. He even gave me a title idea: The Student. We were stoked. This was our first time we would operate as a production company. We would be able to hire a small crew, do some set design, get a nice lighting package—I was excited.

They were flying in from Connecticut, and we were set to shoot the whole thing in a day and then they'd fly out that night or early in the morning. I came up with a story, and we used my house in Topanga for a set. My brother's business partner, Shawn, can be an intense dude, to say the least. He's a motivated guy who likes to see progress and execution and doesn't like to waste time. This was the first time he'd ever been on a set, and I think it was an eye-opening experience for him, seeing how we shot things out of sequence, day for night, exteriors, interiors, simulating headlights on the windows outside, framing, sound, delays, setup, teardown, movement, blocking, etc. We were operating like a machine, though. However, the amount of setups we were doing was going to take time. Shawn was literally standing over Daniel's and my shoulders, watching the clock tick. Their departing flight was also super early the next morning so they basically were going to get very little sleep. We ended around midnight, but he was ready to be done hours before that. I kept telling him, almost there, almost there, it was like working against a ticking clock, as is the case on most sets.

We finally wrapped and got it all in the can. Shawn thanked us, we tore down the set, and then we celebrated. We drank, smoked, and talked about how intense the day was and how proud we were of everyone who worked that day for us. I was so ramped up, I didn't even realize that the sun was now starting to rise. We watched the sun come up and then everyone parted ways. As the leader of the group, I was proud of my team and proud of my business. It was a good day, and the subsequent short film that was derived from it I believe showcases the amount of hard work and professionalism that was displayed throughout the production.

Josh and I discussed it, and we agreed that it was worth the investment to get an office at AFM that year. Same mentality: If we wanted to play with the big boys, we needed to be where the big boys are. Everyone busted their butts to get ready. I decided we should focus on four films in development; Daniel went to work creating some killer artwork for them; I organized pitch packets, website, business cards, posters, etc.; Josh paid for everything and also was there during the market to help me out. I remember arriving there on the first day and coming out of the elevator and walking down the hall toward our room and seeing RYNORYDER/BOYER PRODUCTIONS on a sign out front. I was fucking proud of us, man. Here we were, not even a year into taking the plunge, and we had a fucking office with our names out front. I was excited to step out and make a name for ourselves.

I worked the market and Josh did his thing. Daniel was there for one of the days and got to taste it a bit. We were all in the same mind-set of "This is it." I think the people around us could sense it too. I'll get around to talking about what exactly came out of AFM that year in a bit, but it was another success and another notch on the belt for us. We had accomplished what we came there to do. As one of the final days was winding down, Josh and I sat in our office, had some drinks, and watched *Evidence*. Even though I have seen that movie more times that anyone else in the world, it still gives me a sense of pride and inspiration when I watch it. Kind of like a calling card of, "You can do this, Ryan. You've made a movie before; you can do it again." That was another good day.

This final memory is more of the same, I guess. It was mid-December and we had our first official RynoRyder/Boyer Christmas party. We had dinner at a nice place in Redondo Beach. Daniel and I brought our wives. Josh worked for the company that owned the restaurant, so the meal was comped. We ate, we drank, we smoked. We laughed, we reminisced, and we talked about the future and told imaginary stories of five years from now, with us continuing this Christmas party tradition.

At least, that's what I remember. Turns out that not everyone experienced the same confidence and good vibes I had. Was I manic again? Was I delusional? I don't think so, yet I don't know. My blessing and my curse is my ability to inspire others, to lead others. Now when people tell me I'm an inspiration to them or tell me they look up to me in any way, it makes me very uncomfortable inside. This is something I will have to learn to deal with. I don't say the things I say to inspire others. I say what I say because it's my truth. My ambitions rest upon an extremely tall and near-impossible mountain to climb, and I'm not just talking about golden fucking statues. I'm talking about changing the game for the better, forever. Through complete chaos and anarchy will the cream then rise to the top, without the boundaries or gates that my industry has somehow put up to others over its 100 years or so existence.

I can't say for certain how everyone else felt that night, but I was so fucking confident in my team that had been assembled. I knew there was nothing that could stop us. I later found out there *was* one thing that could bring this all to a screeching halt—me.

"I am the rock,

I am the pillar.

I am the saint,

I am the sinner.

I have the power to create and the power to destroy equally.

Am I Jekyll or am I Hyde?

It's too hard to choose, so I'll let all of YOU decide."

CHAPTER EIGHT: TUESDAY, MARCH 28, 2017

All right…now the good stuff. Or, the completely bat-shit-crazy horrible stuff. However you want to look at it.

It's finally time for me to walk you through the events leading up to the night of March 28, 2017, as well as the night itself. It is a night that has changed my life forever. As with everything else I've written in this book, what I'm going to tell you now is 100% true. It's not a hunch, it's not what I think—it's what happened to me. Let me set it up.

Through our efforts at AFM, we had made some contacts and got interest to finally make our first movie as a production company and that movie was going to be *Evidence: Ground Zero,* the follow-up to the first film *Evidence.* I believe that franchise to be cursed, and I just didn't feel the connection to directing it again. I wrote the script, and I'd produce the hell out of it, but I wanted someone else to direct it. I chose to have Daniel direct and DP. The company we were partnering with agreed, and I gave Daniel free rein to go back through the script and give it a solid rewrite. He was hammering away at that, and we were making some great progress.

It was now sometime in February, and I noticed something happening, both to me and around me. I had begun to read books for the first time in say 20 years. One of these books was about a psychiatrist who specialized in hypnosis and specifically studied past lives. The book is composed of about 60 or so interviews that the author conducted. I found it to be fascinating. Now let me tell you, something inside me has always told me I was meant for something big. I have since mapped out the dates and events and people that have been involved in my life, and am confident now that the signs I grew up seeing were true.

I'm having a difficult time finding the right words to explain myself, but I'll continue to try.

Something started to take over my brain. I've always seen signs throughout my life, mostly numbers, the clock reading 11:11, things of that nature. I'm sure most of you have experienced similar things. I would usually see a sign here and there about once a week, once every other week. Now began to see them every 10 minutes. Music, lights flickering, numbers, license plates, people's birthdays, certain songs playing, people saying things I already knew they were going to say—basically, I found the universe speaking to me, and it was freaking me the fuck out. It felt as though my mind was turning into a much more heightened state. I started researching as much as I could online about other people who see signs. A lot of physics, angel numbers (just Google it, mom!), that sort of stuff. The book I was reading also talked about it. Everything in the world, the very reason for my existence, began to come clear to me, but there was still a layer of fog surrounding it.

I felt that I was compelled to tell a story of literal Biblical proportions and include every moral fiber of good and bad that mankind is capable of and adding it to the themes and characters I was building. I started outlining. I'll include pictures of my office from that time, but I was going through stacks of Post-it Notes, paper, tape, markers, pens. I basically locked myself in my office every minute of every day, outlining this story. For a week or more, I didn't interact with my family. I would sleep four hours and then wake up at 2 am and work until 7 am then sleep for a couple more hours, then wake up and keep working. I was scaring the shit out of Abi because I wasn't telling her anything. I couldn't tell her anything because I knew what was happening would sound ridiculous. I believe the universe was tapping into me, tasking me with the job of retelling the Bible. The world is in such a shift right now that we as human beings have lost our perspective on life and we need to be slapped across the face. I wanted to build a machine of sorts and a platform where I could tell this story to every living human on the planet, and I believed I had discovered a mathematical formula for happiness. I'm not joking. And I'm not necessarily wrong either.

I had the story broken down into seven parts, just like the seven days of creation from the Book of Genesis. The weather was out of control that week. It was pouring down rain and windy, and I knew why. This was my flood. I worked with such fear and anxiety because the more and more I worked, the more and more signs I was seeing. I was literally talking with spirits. I know what a medium feels like now. It was overwhelming to say the least. It was a constant barrage of voices advising me and pointing me in the direction I was meant to go. The cross I was set to bear. The things I was meant to accomplish in this life were and are incredible. I would not wish this upon any other person. It's too great a burden to carry. Now, let me tell you why I will do it, and anytime it gets hard, I think about the message I received that night.

Abi finally had enough. I told her I just needed Daniel to come up and see what I was working on. I needed to explain everything to him and I also knew he was an important part of the puzzle, I just didn't know how exactly. I thought I was going to have him come up to the house and I'd show him everything and it would all click to him. He agreed to come up and I proceeded to walk him through everything. He looked at me like I was a fucking lunatic. We got into a screaming match at each other outside. Abi came out to see what the hell was going on. I can only imagine what was going through Abi's poor mind that week and in those days leading up to everything.

Daniel finally calmed me down and explained to me I was being manic. That it's okay. Abi left for work, and Daniel convinced me to take everything down for the sake of my marriage. I documented everything with pictures and videos on my phone and tore it all down, but I didn't forget the message. I still was going to tell this story somehow, but I just needed to at least "act" sane for my wife. This was about the end of February.

Things calmed down for me, and I began to put my energy into more positive things like doing YouTube videos for KidNaCanyon or working on *Ground Zero*. My head was still spinning and the signs didn't stop, but I forced myself into normalcy, at least the sense of it on the outside.

My mom came down to stay with us for Canon's birthday, March 24. The company we were making *Ground Zero* with didn't like the changes Daniel was making to the script, and we kept going back and forth until finally, they just asked if I would do the rewrite and include a couple ideas of Daniel's in there. Daniel and I began working together on the script. I remember one night when my mom was staying with us and Abi was at work, Daniel and I were in my office working on the script. We were crushing it. After Daniel left, I stayed up and talked with my mom as I always do. My relationship with my mom is one free of judgement and filled with honesty. I told my mom some of the things that were racing around in my mind. I remember walking her up to the guest trailer we have on the property that night, still wide-eyed and rambling about how I believed the universe was trying to tell me something and I believed I was meant for some great purpose. She said, "Who do you think you are? Jesus?" I don't remember how it happened, but I had cut both my palms somehow a few days earlier, and there were still marks on my hands. The timing was ironic as I showed her the two cuts on my palms and said, "I don't know, you tell me," It looked just like the images I'd grown up with of the hands of Jesus after his resurrection. She said something like, "Oh, boy...."

I told her goodnight and remember walking back to my house shaking my head thinking, I can't believe this is really happening. The conversation with my mom left me believing that something like the universe talking to you could happen. My mom has been a devout Catholic her entire life and worked for the church for 30+ years. She shared with me moments she's experienced that were unexplainable, but these were mostly ghosts or things of that nature. What I was trying to get across is that I believed "God" was speaking directly to me. I no longer use the term God, but for those of you who pray to God, or any god for that matter, it's easier to understand and comprehend. I now say universe, because I don't know what else to call it. I've found in my studies since that most Eastern philosophy believes in the same thing. That we are all connected, everything on this planet and everything in our known universe.

Okay, let's get this over with.

By the time March 28 rolled around, things had leveled out in the house. Abi was no longer afraid of how I was acting, we just had a successful birthday with Canon and family and friends, and the progress Daniel and I were making on the script was going great. That day, Daniel was going to come up to the house, and he and I were going to work on the script together. We worked on it for probably about four hours and found a great rhythm and made some really great progress. It was about eight o'clock and Daniel and I decided to call it a day and go sit around the fire pit, smoke some weed, have a glass of wine, and talk about our future plans as a company. So, that's exactly what we did.

We talked about our plans for *Ground Zero*, we talked about other scripts I had and other projects we were doing and who was going to do what on them. Which ones we would do first, who'd direct, who we'd get to produce, which actors we'd get to play, just happy talk. I noticed Bruce and Sandy were in the hot tub as I walked back inside to get another glass of wine. They live in a quaint guest house on the property. Canon was already asleep in his room and Abi was relaxing on the couch, watching her TV shows. I offered to pour her a glass of wine as well, and she was happy she didn't have to get up herself to do it. She asked what we were doing and I told her we're all good, Daniel and I are just hanging out and talking. She was happy she got some time to herself. I gave her the glass of wine and kissed her on the lips and said I was going back outside. It was about 9:30 or so at night. The next time Abi would see me, I would be naked and bursting through my office door trying to get into Canon's room.

That's fucking crazy to think about.

I remember as I walked back down to the fire pit, the wind swirled in the trees and I felt what I had been referring to as Alex. It was a spirit, guiding me, giving me signals. Let me give you some context. Before Abi and I ever met, she had a best friend named Alex who tragically died in a plane crash in the Pacific Ocean. Abi could feel her presence when she went to the beach, and I started to find myself feeling as though I knew Alex as well. During the manic Post-it phase, I even told Abi that I believed the reason Alex died was so that she would help guide me in what I had to do. Abi wasn't happy and said how dare I use her friend and her tragic death as a reason for me doing anything. I believe she said, "Shame on you." I now know that this "Alex" spirit I feel is just a wiser soul guiding me, but it 100% has a female aura to it. For ease of writing, I'll refer to this spirit as Alex from now on.

So as I walked down, Alex made her presence known. Anytime she shows up, I get a sense of happiness, beauty, and love, all encased in a wonderful blue light. I sat back down at the fire pit and gave Daniel his refill of wine and sat down. It was shortly after this that Daniel told me he had always wanted to do a big *Game of Thrones*-style, epic TV show, all based around the life of David. Like, David from the Bible, David. Really the only story I knew of him was the one everyone knows, the story of David and Goliath. Daniel, an atheist, had always had a fascination with this story and had read the Bible several times and knew it well. He grew up in the Bible Belt of Texas and was made to read and study the Bible. Daniel asked me if I knew the story, and I told him what I just told you, and he asked me if I wanted to hear it. That's when a voice entered my head and said, SAY YES. I'm going to write this voice in all caps because the words I was receiving from that moment on were as clear as ALL CAPS are on a page.

Daniel began telling me the story of David. Darkness surrounded my vision and made it tunnel-like. The voice said to me, PAY ATTENTION. LISTEN AND UNDERSTAND WHAT YOU ARE ABOUT TO HEAR. IT'S IMPORTANT. Now, at this point, I'm internally freaking the fuck out. I'd seen signs, had coincidences happen, connected the dots through numbers, always knew I was meant for something great, but I had never had this happen to me before. A voice that sounds both strangely familiar and almost like your own, yet completely different in every way. It was like someone talking to you over a headset. You can hear it loud and clear, but there's no one around whose mouth you can put the voice to. My point is, even though I had never heard this voice before, I could trust it.

I curled up in my chair and wrapped myself in my sweater. This sweater that I put on every morning when I wake up now was bought by Abi at a clothing store in Topanga years ago. WRAP YOURSELF IN YOUR SWEATER. IT WILL PROTECT YOU AND SHIELD YOU FROM WHAT YOU ARE ABOUT TO EXPERIENCE. FIND COMFORT IN IT IF YOU BECOME TOO FRIGHTENED BY WHAT'S ABOUT TO HAPPEN.

Daniel began telling me things I had no idea about David. I still don't know specifics, nor do I want you to think I'm some Bible expert, but Daniel knew his story inside and out. Things began happening. As Daniel was telling the story of David, I was correlating things to my own life and what is going to happen in the future. I've never been more scared in my life. DON'T WORRY. YOU HAVE PROTECTION HERE. WHAT IS HAPPENING IS REAL. YOU NEED TO GET THROUGH THIS, THOUGH. I KNOW YOU'RE SCARED. At this point, Bruce and Sandy got out of the hot tub. They didn't say any words at all. Nothing. Instead, Bruce walked up behind me and rubbed the back of my ears. He had never done that to me before in seven years of knowing him, nor has he done it since, *nor* do I think he'll ever do it again. But his message was clear. WE'RE HERE FOR YOU. YOU'RE SAFE. NOW LISTEN. And then they walked inside their house. I moved chairs to sit closer to Daniel, and he proceeded with the story.

Every time I couldn't match a place in the story to a place in my own life or a character in David's story with someone who was in *my* life, Daniel would all of a sudden lose his train of thought. He would say something like he suddenly couldn't remember where he was going. He knew this story so well, he couldn't believe he would suddenly forget things. What he didn't know is that it was because I wasn't making the connection. GOT IT? DO YOU UNDERSTAND THIS PART? DO YOU SEE THE CONNECTION? I would be in my head, bouncing to different cities that I knew or parts of the world or people, both private and public. NO. NO. YES, THAT'S IT. NOW, CONTINUE TO LISTEN. Daniel would suddenly remember where he'd left off and continue with the story. This happened probably four to six times.

I was becoming emotional and so was Daniel. We both had tears in our eyes. We would stop and check in on each other to see if we both were good. I told Daniel something was happening and asked if he felt it too. He said yes. I told him we had to get through this together, that he had to finish the story so that I could hear everything. I may have mentioned to him the reason I knew he would lose his train of thought—I think I did but I could be wrong. The voice didn't stop and other things began happening. The voice knew I was scared and wanted protection. SEVEN SPIRITS. THERE ARE SEVEN SPIRITS HERE FOR YOUR PROTECTION. THEY WERE ALL BROUGHT HERE FOR THIS VERY MOMENT. I quickly ran through everything and did the math. 1.) Abi. 2.) Canon. 3.) Bruce. 4.) Sandy. 5.) Daniel. 6.) Alex. But who was the seventh? I thought it was me. Then, I felt the seventh come through. NO, IDIOT. IT'S ME. THIS IS WHY I ENTERED YOUR LIFE, TO BE HERE FOR YOU IN THIS MOMENT. 7.) Dutch.

When I made this connection, I started to let go. I took everything in. The wind was swirling and the fire turned blue on command. I was literally able to conjure it to happen at will. I even made Daniel stop telling the story and showed him I was able to control the wind as well. It was the most unbelievable thing I've ever seen or felt. Daniel and I kept saying to each other we couldn't believe what was going on and how is this possibly happening? I pushed Daniel to finish. I knew I needed to hear the rest of it so I could see all of the plans that were to be laid out for me. Then, I heard YOU MUST THREATEN DANIEL. HE WILL BETRAY YOU AT SOME POINT AND YOU NEED TO EXPERIENCE THAT EMOTION RIGHT NOW. I was crying by that point and I said, "No! I can't! I don't want to!" YOU MUST DO THIS. NOW. That's when I leapt out of my chair and jumped on top of Daniel. I grabbed his throat and raised my fist in the air. This was the first time my voice changed. This *felt* different inside. I can only imagine what it sounded like to someone else, but I knew it wasn't my voice.

I calmed back down and sat back in my chair. I told Daniel it was okay, that he needs to keep going. Daniel refused. He said he didn't know what the fuck was going on, but he was done. I calmly, with tears in my eyes, begged for him to finish. I needed to go through this all, tonight, right now in this moment. Daniel finally agreed and continued to tell the story of David.

I found myself hitting a wall. No matter how many times Daniel tried to explain the story to me, I felt that there was something holding me back from getting to the next part. And then I got my answer how. YOU NEED TO GIVE YOURSELF UP. SURRENDER YOUR BODY. YOU NEED TO DIE. I lost it. I cried, screamed out, "*Nnnooo!!!*" But the voice persisted. THIS IS WHAT YOU ARE MEANT TO DO. IF YOU GIVE IN NOW, YOU WILL HELP THE

WORLD. IT MUST BE DONE. IT'S UP TO YOU. I started to consider it. I went through in my head what that really meant. It's easy to say you'd die for someone or something, but when that moment actually presents itself and you know you're going to die and you have the time to think about what that really means, this is something I never wish anyone ever has to go through.

I, of course, first said goodbye to Abi and Canon. I thought I would be around a little longer to see Canon grow up, but the voice told me what *his* role in all of this is, and let me tell you, he will live with far less suffering, but he will have an incredibly large mantel to carry on. Listen to me when I tell you, I am not going to live long enough to see absolutely everything that needs to change happen. However, Canon's children will. If I'm the first wave, Canon is the cavalry that will clean everything up. I was told there would be a daughter as well.

After comprehending as best I could that I was going to die, I told the voice I was scared and not ashamed to admit that. All it said was TRUST ME. GIVE IN. WE WILL TAKE CARE OF YOU. So..........I did it. I let go. In my head, I died.

I tore off all of my clothes and dropped onto the ground and stared up at the night sky. I screamed at the top of my lungs, "*Taaaakkkkeee Mmmeeeee!!!!*" I repeated it over and over and over again. Daniel was frantic, pleading for me to keep quiet. It was nearing midnight by now and I knew how loud I was being, but the voice assured me that no one would hear it. I was safe and in a bubble. Canon wouldn't wake up, Bruce and Sandy wouldn't. The neighbors wouldn't hear. WE WILL HIDE IT IN THE BREEZE. IT WILL SOUND LIKE THE WIND BLOWING TO THEM. So I didn't stop. I felt something, an energy, a force, from my chest. I watched it burst out of me and leave. It went up into the sky and I was gone. There was only one thing that entered my mind then. The last piece of the puzzle. The final thing I needed to complete on this magical night. GET TO CANON.

Like a switch, I stopped convulsing and screaming. I quickly stood up and made a bee line for the house. My destination was Canon, who was sleeping in his bedroom. I didn't know why I had to do it, I just knew that it would all end if I could get to him. It told me I needed to strip myself of all possessions. Most of my clothes were already off, but I even had to take off my Grandpa's necklace I wear every day and throw that aside as well. Nothing. I had to go back to zero.

Okay...let's take a step back and talk about what was happening right now outside of what was going on in my head and body. The last time Abi saw me was almost two hours ago when I came inside and poured her a glass of wine and gave her a kiss. It was a Tuesday night, for fuck's sake. If you've just read these paragraphs and you think it's all bullshit, please let me know, because I'm still to this day having a hard time completely believing all of it. I have a saying when people ask me about that night of 90/10. Ninety percent of me knows and understands that I was in a manic time period, unmedicated, undiagnosed, and that the human brain is capable of far more than any of us will probably ever fully know or understand.

However, there is still 10% of my brain that can't deny hearing that VOICE and it telling me my future. I just can't. It's literally the reason why I now wake up every single day of my life and work my face off to accomplish this one goal of changing the world for the better. I mean, I was told by SOMETHING what my purpose in life was. That doesn't happen to everyone. I understand how valuable and how precious a thing that is, and I refuse to let it go or waste it. I could just have easily said no. What I'm going to face in my life and the mountain I have to climb is going to be really, really fucking difficult. It told me that. I made the conscious choice to accept the burden and to carry my cross because let me tell you this, what's waiting for us on the other side is truly the most beautiful thing I've ever experienced and it is filled with nothing but love and good. Now, back to the action.

Abi heard me screaming and walked outside to see what was going on. I blew right past her and threw the back sliding door open and entered my office. Daniel came running up behind me and told Abi he thinks they needed to call 911. Abi was completely confused. My closet door that led from my office to the rest of the house was closed. During the "Post-it phase" weeks earlier, I had put a piece of paper above that door that said Family. I was told to put it there as a reminder to me that when I left my office, I left to be with my family and I couldn't bring what was happening inside my office out into the real world. I mean, I was talking to spirits out loud, people. My point is, I chuckled to myself as I saw that door, the sign since removed, because at that time the only thing important in my head *was* my family. It was just one of many other signals or signs I received throughout that night that told me everything would be okay and that this was meant to happen and, more importantly, *needed* to happen. So I crashed through the door like the Hulk.

Here's where things get nuts. I'm going to just list off what I think happened next. I know all of my actions are true; I'm just a bit hazy as to the exact order in which they happened, but I think it went something like this.

I went straight for Canon's bedroom and I don't know if it was here or later, but Abi stood in front of the door like a mother lion and wouldn't let me get to him. I grabbed her by the throat, possibly choked her, raised a fist, definitely pushed her, I think I probably hit her, not super hard—either way, she wasn't letting me in. Daniel came in and said he thought they should call 911. Abi said of *course* they should call 911 and what the fuck happened?? I was in the hallway and Daniel now came and tried to restrain me. At some point I went into the kitchen. I heard someone say, "Bath salts." I chuckled again because Daniel and I had just been talking about bath salts in the *Ground Zero* script and I took it as another sign. I then dropped to the ground and did my best impression of what I thought someone on bath salts would look like.

I twisted and contorted my body. I was screaming out a guttural noise. I was flexing my throat like a frog or toad. I was crawling around on the kitchen tile spewing red saliva. I crawled across the living room and headed for Canon's room again. Daniel held me down in the hallway on the floor. I stopped struggling and resisting. Let me go back.

As insanely crazy and possessed as I would act, I would snap out of it and have these moments of real consciousness and calmness. I understood everything that was happening around me and would speak in a very calm and soft tone. I would see something or get another sign or signal, and I would drift off into this fourth dimension of time and space.

So by this time, I was on the floor of the hallway. Daniel asked me if I wanted a blanket. I was butt naked and shivering and said yes. He opened the hallway closet where we keep towels and blankets and there was my University of Texas Longhorns blanket that Abi's mom had made and given to me. It was a sign. I told him yes, that one, and wrapped myself around in it. I thought it would help protect me.

It was around this time that I got up and was guided to sit down on the couch, and that's when I saw my house was filled with police officers and paramedics. The news was on TV in the background and I remember my very first thought and the first thing out of my mouth was, "Oh, fuck...am I on the news?" Let me explain, I live in Los Angeles and we are notorious for helicopter news coverage in LA. I was pretty sure I hadn't done anything *that* terrible or crazy, but then there was this other part of me that was like, dude...you've lost your fucking mind. You could have done something so disastrous that it might have made the news. I did think that would have been pretty cool on one level if I did.

So I made it to the couch and one of the paramedics started talking to me. I can only imagine how I sounded to these strangers. I was convinced that the farther away from Canon's room I went, the more the pain would come back. That's the best way for me to explain it. I even told them, in a very calm manner, "Go ahead, just try and move me. Watch what happens. As soon as my body goes through that doorway leading through my office and outside, it will come back." I gladly stood up and they would guide me toward the door and I would feel it come back and I would start losing my shit again, screaming and flailing about. They would all panic and get me back on the couch, and it would go away and I'd be completely calm and coherent again. I'd look up at them and smile and say, "See. I told you." This probably happened two or three times, definitely more than once. That's when I saw Abi's Uncle Cavin in the background, behind some other people. I knew he was there as a guide for me. Let me explain.

Abi's Uncle Cavin is an incredibly interesting individual. His spirituality and outlook on life are fascinating. Let's just say, he HAS it, you know? He's a very old soul. He's still very much alive, but for some reason, he appeared to me that night. Well, not for *some* reason, for *a* reason. Because I trusted him so much in real life, when he appeared in this fourth dimension I was going in and out of, I knew I should trust him there too. I ended up on the floor by now. The paramedics were trying to get me out of the house and I was not having it. Cavin told me to listen and to try and do as they ask. I remember a female paramedic, I believe, hearing her say as I lay face down on the floor, "Can we just put you on the gurney here in the living room and not move you?" I heard her, I listened, I processed the information and decided that I'm already lying on the floor, I could lie on a gurney just as easily. It'd be like lying in a bed, and I told her yes.

The next thing I know, those bastards, I'm up on the gurney and they are wheeling me outside. I'm screaming at the top of my lungs but by now the cops had handcuffed both my arms to the metal railings of the gurney. The first time I looked down and saw I was restrained, panic hit. So much fucking panic. Have you ever been restrained like that? Not sexually or anything, but truly chained to something? Both hands unable to even scratch your fucking nose if you have an itch? It's petrifying not being able to move, especially when you're in a state of mind like I was that night.

But every time I would start to lose control, I would look around me for Cavin. I would see him and shout out his name and it was so comforting to me. He told me to listen to them and to go along. I was outside by now, and they were wheeling me toward an ambulance. That's when I saw a black paramedic and I began yelling out the N-word, not in a violent or hateful way, it was more like how I would say it when I was around my friends in high school to try and get a reaction. Thankfully, the dude understood and was even laughing about it. When I saw that, I began dropping the "er" off the end and changed it to an "a," if you all know what I mean. I was shouting out for somebody to contact Christopher Nolan. If you haven't seen *Interstellar*, you might not understand, but that movie explores travelling into the fourth dimension, which I was, and I thought if I could just talk to him, he'd understand what was happening to me.

Abi kills it in the delivery of this next part, but it's too good not to include in this book. As her husband and father of her child is being wheeled out of the house and into an ambulance, screaming God knows what crazy things, she is standing there with Bruce and Sandy, watching. Abi looks at her watch and sees it's past midnight and consequently Sandy's birthday. Abi dead-pans over to her and says, "By the way, happy birthday, Sandy." If anyone knows Abi, they know her dry wit and timing are impeccably hilarious. God, I love that woman...

Okay, let's go inside the ambulance now. I can't be certain when it happened, but at some point I heard a female paramedic say we have to lift him up because I had shit and pissed myself. That made sense because before that, during one of my out-of-body times, the VOICE told me not to be embarrassed by anything and that I must release my body. This was before I heard I had shit myself. I then remember sitting in the ambulance, strapped to the gurney for what seemed like 20 minutes before they closed the doors and we started moving. Let me try and explain what was happening at that time.

I was going in and out of consciousness, but the unconscious state I would go into was in this fourth dimension. I've since talked to people and read interviews or watched videos online of people who have taken hallucinogens like LSD or mushrooms or acid and heard stories of people who have performed some ancient ritual who have had similar effects. I have never even come close to doing a hard drug like that, but that's the best way I can describe the state of mind I would go into. I would suddenly come out of it into the "regular" world, and I would quickly scramble and look for a sign to help guide me and reassure me everything was okay. So I would say the first thing that popped into my head about their appearance or ask them some really personal question about their life or family, store that information, and then willingly go back into the other dimension. Why would I *willingly* go back? Let me tell you why. Because when I did, I lost any and all sense of pain and time. There was so much love on that other side. Plus, it was fun. I would stop time, like *freeze* it. For as long as I wanted. I could rewind something that just happened and then play it out again with different outcomes. If, for example, I panicked or got scared when the ambulance started to drive away, I would go into this other dimension, stop the ambulance, rewind it, play it out again and again until I was comfortable with moving forward, and then allow time to continue moving.

I came back to reality and suddenly realized that we were moving. We must be on the freeway somewhere. I thought about what hospital they would take me to and knew there's one close in Agoura Hills but I had never been there. There was a sheriff's deputy sitting in there with me, near my head. I turned my head up to him and looked him deep in the eyes. I had never experienced anything like that before, but now I do it as much as I can. I was able to see *through* his eyes and into his soul, really. I can't remember what it was, but I asked him something very personal and it almost brought him to tears. I fucking shit you not. I wish I could remember what we talked about. I do remember one thing, though. I asked him what his favorite number was during one of my conscious states to see if I could connect that number with a sign everything was okay. He told me his favorite number was 11. I was filled with such a sense of satisfaction. I said, "Of course it is," with a smile on my face and dipped back into that fourth dimension.

Not sure what took so long, but they kept me in the outside waiting area of the hospital before taking me to a room—I guess one wasn't available for me. I was still going in and out of consciousness at this point. In my head, I was going from realizing I'm alive to convinced I was dead. Hospitals are all white, and I was facing up toward the lights. I've heard some people explain when they died, if their soul needed recharging, they've explained it like being in a hospital—it was just all making complete sense to me, and it's *really* hard to try and put it into words but I'm doing the best I can.

I asked if I could have a room across the way that I saw because it was room 11. I don't know what room number they finally put me in, but it wasn't that one. People were coming up and taking my blood pressure and blood samples. That's when I looked up and saw Cavin. I screamed out with such joy. "Isn't this a fucking trip, Cavin! Can you believe what's happening?" I was sure that Cavin was visiting me in his dreams or somehow to guide me and comfort me. Cavin smiled his sweet smile and said nothing. That's when I watched his face slowly melt and transform into a similar-looking face, but a complete stranger nonetheless. I calmly said, "You're not Cavin, are you?" He shook his head and smiled. I asked if he were at the house and he said yes. I asked him what *his* name was and he told me but I can't remember it. I want to say Hank or something with an "H." It took me a couple more times of going in and out, but eventually I understood that this person was not Cavin, it was "Hank" from "Pittsburg" who had been a paramedic for "ten" years...I tried to ask as much about him as I could so that when he turned back into Cavin and I started calling him Cavin again, when I came back I'd rattle off everything about him to try and ground myself in reality.

They moved me into a room, and the two paramedics who drove me in the ambulance for some reason had to stay in the room with me until the doctor could come and talk to me. I was again going in and out of consciousness, going from the reality of what was actually happening to being 100% convinced that I had died and that my soul needed to heal. I thought, how long are they going to make me stay in here? I then realized time no longer existed. That took me a while to comprehend. I did overhear the two paramedics basically bitching because I was the last call of their shift and they got stuck having to work extra hours. Sorry!

Finally, a doctor came in and talked to me. The first thing I asked him was, "Am I dead?" He said no. I persisted, "You sure I'm not dead?" "No, you're fine. Your blood pressure is a little high and you're dehydrated, but other than that, you're fine. Can you tell me what happened?" Now if you've read all of this up to this point, it's not exactly something you can just rattle off and it's not something everybody can comprehend. I still had no fucking idea what just happened to me, but I remembered everything. I started trying to calmly explain everything I've just told you. Daniel and I were working on the script, sitting around the fire, suddenly a VOICE...I looked at the eyes of everyone in there who was looking at me as I stuttered through my explanation. I could tell they all thought I was full of shit. That's when I started to realize that nobody will ever believe me. They all wrote it off that I was making this all up and were convinced I had a bad trip of acid or LSD or bath salts or something like that.

They finally felt I was safe enough to remove the handcuffs. Man, that was relief. I started to feel myself staying in the conscious world more and more. I noticed that the saner I acted and spoke, the safer everyone else felt and thus felt it okay to let me go. The next couple of hours before they decided to release me were rough, uncomfortable, and so confusing. It was the beginning of me digesting everything that happened to me. I didn't know how else to explain it, other than it was the VOICE of whatever it is that created all of us. How would I possibly be able to explain something like this to Abi?

A nurse finally came in and told me it was okay for me to go. *What*?? I don't have any clothes, not sure where I am, and no money or phone. Were they just going to throw me on the streets? Has anyone notified my wife? I told them I had no way of getting home and could I use a phone? She said there's a free phone in the outside lobby area I could use. I asked if there were any socks or something for my feet. She was sympathetic about my situation, I could tell. She went and got me socks and an extra shirt. I was trembling.

I had to sign out at the front desk. I remember the lady mentioned something about payment and asked if I had insurance and I said no. She said there were some expenses incurred, blood work, fluids, etc. I must have looked like a wet puppy dog when I simply just looked at myself and held my hands up saying, "Look at me. I have nothing." She gave me a look of compassion and nodded her head. "Just go. It's okay." I turned and walked out into the lobby as quickly as I could, hoping that nobody would notice me or say anything. I went to the free phone and called my wife. Abi couldn't believe they were just releasing me like that and also couldn't believe she had to pack up Canon at five in the morning and pick up her husband whom she'd just seen hours before, screaming and flailing about like a lunatic. She was rightfully afraid, but she did it.

I was afraid I'd miss her when she pulled up or she wouldn't see me, so I sat close to the window and kept staring outside. It was still dark. About 20 or 30 minutes later, I recognized my Jeep and I hurried up and walked outside. I can only imagine what was going through her mind when I climbed in the car, still in my hospital gown, shirt and socks. I told her thank you and saw Canon thankfully asleep in the back. I *think* he was asleep, I don't remember much about the ride home. We stayed pretty silent. I think Abi asked briefly what happened to me and all I said was I don't know, because I truly didn't.

We got home and Abi and Canon went to bed. Abi told me she didn't want me to sleep in the bed with her and that I could sleep in Canon's. She was still too afraid. I agreed. I took a nice, warm shower. I still had remnants of piss, shit, and vomit all over me, plus I was freezing. I cleaned up and put on some sweats and a shirt and passed out in Canon's bed—the same place just hours before I tried to burst my way into.

That's it. Every single thing I've written down in this chapter, as with my entire book, is 100% true and accurate to the best of my memories and testimonies. In the next and final chapter, I'll talk about the next calendar year that followed and how I literally declared war on recovery. I'll talk about how that VOICE still has not gone away, but I've learned, or am learning, to control it. If any of what I wrote down made any sense at all, you'll now see why March 28 is a date that will be forever chiseled into my memory. The Ryan McCoy that existed for 36 years died that night. Died. I am no longer the same person.

"The greatest adventure in life begins with you.

Forever a bridge,

Forever a bond.

Cast off and fear not,

For we are always with you."

CHAPTER NINE: THE TOP OF A MOUNTAIN

I woke up a few hours later in Canon's bed. I did nothing that day. I couldn't. Not only was I physically sore from the heaving and growling, but mentally I had no clue who I was anymore. Abi and I didn't talk much about it, and anytime I would try and articulate what happened, I would feel myself amping up and would have to stop. It took quite a while before I was able to talk about that night without being afraid of losing it again. I actually had an appointment scheduled for the next day with a hypnotherapist. There was no way my brain could handle that. I explained briefly what happened and apologized to her. She understood, and I've never thought about going back. There was no need anymore—I had received all the information and answers I needed.

I immediately got on Seroquel, actually the generic version of it, quetiapine, which I still take to this day. I only take one 25-mg pill each night, and it basically just knocks me out. I remember after the first night I took it, Abi asked me if I could tell a difference. The difference, I realized, was that it felt like I was getting actual sleep for the first time in my adult life. Before when I would close my eyes to go to sleep, all I would see were lights and shapes and things and my brain wouldn't stop working. Now when I close my eyes, I don't hear that noise and all I see is black.

The day after my breakdown, I still had all of the script pages with notes hung up in my office. I took pictures of them all and then tore them all down. I couldn't even begin to think about *Evidence* 2 anymore. Life appeared to go back to normalcy. There were some external factors we had to deal with. I broke Daniel that night. He definitely wasn't recovering and was texting Abi and Josh, telling them I needed to step away from the project and that Abi needed to step in to help produce, and we can't let the company we're doing the movie with find out about this, and on and on. Basically not giving two fucks about my health or well-being. Josh, on the other hand, only cared about my health and well-being. There's a reason Josh is still standing next to me to this day. He is one of the most loyal people I have ever met.

While Daniel was freaking out behind the scenes, I told everyone that I 100% agreed with him, that I should have nothing to do with the project right now, at least as far as getting the script ready. Daniel would handle that. But I still had this urge to be creative. It was scary to me because my brain hadn't stopped firing on all pistons. I didn't tell anyone really, and I hid that creativity by doing more KidNaCanyon videos or building a chicken coop out of spare pieces of wood lying around the property. Then I turned toward writing. And let me tell you something, it was one of the most therapeutic things I could have possibly done. I understood now that basically all my life, I had been writing from the outside in. I'd never actually put *myself*, what I thought and felt, into a character or story. I would give characteristics of mine to characters, but never got to the heart of them. This time I did.

I decided to rewrite one of my screenplays. However, the inspiration started to take over and when I finally gave it to Abi, she said, "This isn't a rewrite, it's a sequel." I told you she always has the best ideas. I looked at it and said you're right. So, I decided to write a third and make it into a trilogy. I don't think there's a character I've written that I love more than the main character, John, who's in the third script. I dug deep inside me and filled that character with everything I have in me. Once I finished those, and I'm talking detailed outlines, several drafts, real work, I decided well, I might as well write *Evidence* 3 and have that ready, which is what I did. In that calendar year, along with everything else I did, I wrote six screenplays, edited a 300+ page book, hand-wrote a 100+ page treatment for another script, and wrote this book. That's what I call ULTRA-creative.

I also read seven or eight books. I hadn't read a book really in 20 years prior to this—now I couldn't stop myself. But I only read nonfiction and mostly older philosophical material. *The Art of Happiness, The Art of War, Meditations*, anything I could get my hands on that would teach me how to become the greatest person I possibly could. Let me give you an analogy if I'm not making sense.

Imagine a large vase. That vase had been full of rocks. Those rocks were who I thought I was. After that night, I realized that my vase wasn't even *close* to being full. I realized I could fit smaller rocks in there, pebbles, sand—the vase had so many other spaces to become full. That's what I was doing. Filling my vase. I also knew the burden I was set to bear in life because I hadn't forgotten the VOICE from that night. I needed to read great works by great men because that's now what I strive to be every single day.

The other major thing I started to do was running. I had been doing it already—it's not like it was something totally new to my routine—but I started to become religious about it. I call it Plug In to Plug Out. I would build playlists on my phone for each of the scripts I was writing. If I had something to figure out in the story, I would put that playlist on and go running. Now, this isn't just your ordinary run. Sure, some of the times I would drive down to Calabasas and run the surface streets, but the one route that's the most spiritual for me is in my backyard. We live in the canyons and there's a horse trail that leads to the top of a mountain. It's a hard climb and I go as fast as I can up that hill.

A couple months after my breakdown, I was feeling really good. Abi and I were in a good place, I was properly medicated, I was kicking ass creatively—all was good. I want to say it was a Sunday, Abi had to go into work, and Bruce and Sandy were gone. About an hour before Abi has to go to work, she and I will sometimes snap at each other for stupid reasons. Deep down it's because she doesn't want to go to work and I don't want her to leave either. So, she'll usually say something that will piss me off, or I'll take it the wrong way and I'll say something smart-ass back to her. Little tiffs anyone married for more than five years knows about. We got into a little tiff just before she had to leave for work at 4 pm. Common human behavior; it's easier to say goodbye to someone you love if you are mad at each other. It makes the pain of your loved one leaving easier to cope with.

It was a nice day outside, and I spent the next two or three hours playing with Canon outside. We had music playing, swung on the swings, I think I even did a KidNaCanyon video with him. By the way, if you don't know what KidNaCanyon is, it's a YouTube channel built for him. Google it.

After we played outside, we came in, I made him dinner, gave him a bath, and he was lights out asleep 15 minutes after I put him to bed. I was feeling great about myself, proud as a dad of the quality time spent with my son, and completely forgot about the tiff with Abi and smiled at the thought of her return. I made myself a cocktail, sat down on the couch, and started watching TV. It was early summer so it was still very light outside. We have a long driveway leading up to our house, and I saw some people walking up. I quickly did the math that no one else was on the property, but sometimes people get lost and come up to ask for directions, so I didn't think much of it, got up, and went to meet them at the back door. I was surprised when I saw three sheriff's deputies standing outside.

My heart is actually racing again right now as I retell this story.

I opened the door and asked them what the problem was. They said, "Did you get in a fight with your wife?" I was fucking stunned. By this time, Abi had been gone to work for over three hours. Where the hell did *this* come from? Suddenly, I was right back to that night. I panicked because I didn't want to lie so I told them about the tiff. They said, "Didn't we have to come up here a few weeks ago?" I was obviously on the cops' radar now. They knew I was crazy. Then they told me they needed to come inside to make sure there wasn't a body. I shit you not.

I backed away as they came inside. I was feeling so fucking violated. They started asking questions, and I tried answering them, but my brain was frantic. Two of the officers were calm and cool, but this one FAT FUCK. YES, IF YOU EVER READ THIS AND KNOW WHO YOU ARE, YOU ARE A FAT FUCKING PIECE OF SHIT. Anyway, this FAT FUCK kept pushing me and I snapped. I got right up in his face and told him, "You REEEAALLLY want to PUSH me, BRO?!?!" I was so pissed that these cops were fucking questioning the safety of my wife and kid! Where were they for the last three hours? Had they shown up even 30 minutes prior, they would have seen me giving my son a bath. Like, what the fuck was going on?

By the grace of God, I wasn't detained, arrested, didn't shove one of them, or punch that FAT FUCK in the face. They apologized, but not without lecturing me on my drinking.

After they finally left, I was broken again. I tried to maintain myself, but I could feel the water in my pot boiling over. My first thought was Abi called the cops on me to get back at me for what I said during our tiff. That was the only explanation I could think of. I called, texted, ASAP. She called back and the first words out my mouth were, "Please tell me you called the cops on me and it wasn't the neighbors." I won't get into it because they've now since moved, but I butted heads with the neighbors in the past. She said no, of course not, and I frantically told her what happened. Abi was just as confused as I was. She had to get back to work and I paced around the house, debating whether or not to go ask the neighbors. Finally, I wrote my full name and both phone numbers there are for me on a piece of paper and stormed next door.

They were in the backyard, having dinner or something. I knocked on the gate and they welcomed me to come in. I said no, I'm fine right here. The woman got up and came up to me. I asked her if she called the cops on me and she said, "Yes." My throat dropped and before she could even start to tell me her reasons for it, I handed her the paper, hand shaking, and told her if she ever has any concerns again to please call us first if she's worried and then turned around and stormed back to my house.

I slammed the sliding door closed behind me and I lost it. I cried all night long. For the next three to four hours, I couldn't stop. I was crying because I was so mad. I was mad at myself for not being able to keep it together. I was mad that I was now on the cops' radar. I was mad that my brain didn't work like other peoples'. I was brought back to the fragility I had during the night of my mental breakdown. I was reliving everything over again. I was suffering from PTSD. That was a bit of a crippling blow, but I was determined to win. And when I say win, I mean win at life; to be happy, to be a good husband, to be a good father, to be a good man.

* * *

I mentioned I built a chicken coop—we obviously had chickens. They were young, and we were concerned the hawks would scoop them up. Then something strange happened: a raven began to show up on our property. Ravens, if you don't know, keep hawks away. This thing is huge and it wasn't like you could go outside and it was always there—this thing would show up out of nowhere and land right in front of you, at least it did for me. It walked and squawked with a smugness that reminded me of something I had seen before…it reminded me of Dutch. He'd come back.

Now if you're reading this part and you think that's crazy then I've already lost you. If you read that and think it's possible, then continue on.

This Raven began showing up during my runs. The rock I climb up on and stand on top of is the highest point of the mountain, save for one other rock about 50 feet away. I've only been to the top of that one once before. It's not easy and it's dangerous as fuck. The only way to get up there is to literally rock climb up a wall on the back side, and if you fall, you fall 80 feet down into a gully. For whatever reason, this one time all alone (stupid), I climbed to the top. There's actually a perfect little area to comfortably sit. You can go the less sketchy way to get back down, but I still had to jump like 12 feet down into a clump of shrubs and got all cut up. But I have been there. Since then I've tried three or four times to climb back up there. I don't think I'll ever try again. It's now the raven's perch and I have mine. The one Raven has now grown into an unkindness of six. But the biggest one, the leader, still serves as a guide to me.

It's hard to put into words without sounding completely cheesy, but the feeling I get when I interact with the Raven is the same feeling I got when I would interact with Dutch. Okay, let me put it this way…Abi knows me better than I know myself. That's easy enough for people to understand. There was something about Dutch that I always knew, I always felt and understood *and* respected, just like I do with Abi, that Dutch always knew me better than I knew myself. That's the feeling I have with this Raven. He never asks for anything, he doesn't want anything from me, but he knows how much deep down I look toward him as a guide. Like, this bird straight up motivates me. Ask my friend who sometimes I'll go running with. His name is JB, and he'll appreciate the shout-out. He knows about the Raven and sure as shit, he's seen these Ravens on our runs show up at very strange yet inspiring moments.

Sometimes I think, perhaps I am giving something in return to these Ravens. Maybe they look forward to seeing me as much as I look forward to seeing them. Yes, other people hike this trail, but no one as often as me and *definitely* not with as much heart and fervor. Is it possible that they feel and feed off of the positive energy my body is resonating during my runs? I told you, I plug in to plug out. What that means is that I've trained my brain and my body to go into a meditative state while performing an excruciatingly physical activity. In theory, it's no different than yoga, I suppose. Animals feed off energy. Hell, every single thing on this *planet* feeds off energy. It's about opening up your mind to that not just possibility, but TRUTH, that I believe you can begin to find real happiness.

This chapter is probably the most difficult. I'm trying to put into words things that I feel and that I know, yet they can't be measured. And there is no immediate return. I began to really open myself to nature. I try and put myself in their place. I try and feel what they would feel. Let me give you this one example.

There is a fire road trail I like to go running on, and there's a hilltop that overlooks the valley and points northwest toward Ventura. It's actually the location we used for my short film, *The Hooker*. A few months back, we had the largest wildfire in California state history. It burned something like 400,00 to 500,000 acres of trees. The entire city had a smoky grayness to it. I was going for a run one day, and I always end my run there by holding onto the branches of a large bush and close my eyes and meditate. The largest section of fires was in Ventura County. Standing there at the top of that mountain, I held onto that branch and looked out at all the destruction. I felt the pain this bush I was holding onto had felt being forced to watch nature burn. We humans are not rooted to any one part of this Earth, but a tree is. It can't move once it is grown. If you believe that trees and plants have energy and spirits connected with them, it's a sobering idea to hold. But putting my mind in that place showed me how fortunate we are as human beings. If we see something we don't like, we can turn away or close our eyes. This tree up here was forced to watch others like it burn.

* * *

It was Christmas 2017 by now. I was back and firing on all cylinders. A story fell into my lap, a true story about a couple dealing with their daughter's drug addiction for 10 years, and I took it as a sign. I won't get into the specifics of why, but let's just say I knew this world and everyone in it. I was meant to tell this story. I put an obnoxiously huge amount of time into it. I'm very proud of it. During this time, Josh and I were drifting further apart. As my confidence and excitement were building, Josh was getting in a lower and lower place. I didn't think he'd be around much longer. He spent Christmas Day alone that year, and I didn't even *think* of inviting him to Abi's brother's house, and he would have been more than welcome. Josh, I'm sorry for that.

January came about, and I had been noodling the idea of starting a podcast/Internet show. When I finally told Abi about it, she said, "It's not a *bad* idea…" A 50% yes from Abi for me is all I needed and I was off to the races.

I made the decision that I would release the first episode on March 28, 2018. Exactly one year to the date of my mental breakdown. I thought if I was able to pull that off, along with everything else I accomplished in that year, I could stick it to the part of my brain I hate and prove that it doesn't define me—I define my own fucking path and that path is clear in my head.

I needed help. I met with Josh and I told him what my plan was. Fuck Hollywood. It almost killed me and my family, and it's driving a wedge between my friendship with Josh. I was going to do a 180 and stop chasing that alluring tail of the Hollywood dragon and put my message out there and go straight digital. I told Josh, I don't have a specific job for you, I just need a friend by my side.

I turned my camera on and pointed it *at* me instead of away from me. It was uncomfortable at first, but I didn't care. I began posting videos on YouTube, Facebook, and just about everywhere else you can. I sent out emails to local colleges offering to give a free talk at their school. I got one hit back and I gave a talk in front of 50 to 60 students at USC and filmed it and put it online. I told these students that I wanted to reach out to the next generation of filmmakers and lend my hand and help guide them through the troughs of my industry and help them not make the same mistakes or fall into the same pitfalls that I had. I also simultaneously plan on destroying Hollywood and eliminating the need for the term "celebrity." Let's talk about this for a second because when I say I've declared war, I want to be clear.

First of all, we need to establish that there is a problem. And I'm going to go straight to the metaphysical because that's the real reason I am doing what I do. I'm following the message I received that night. That message is that I have to build a "machine" over the next 20 to 30 years that, when deployed, will completely take away the need for anyone to ever have the need for a major studio's involvement. How do I know this? Because of my knowledge of the industry and its trending lack of innovation in storytelling, along with the lack of knowledge by all of the top executives about what is happening in the *digital* world—the two paths are going to intersect each other, and if I time my "machine" right, when that moment happens, the game is over. Now, let's talk about why.

Unless you've had your head in the sand over the last two years, you probably feel like some shit's about to go down. If you are empathic in any way, you probably feel like a pendulum shift in humanity is happening. On a technology front, a pendulum shift is *already* happening. And whatever technology you see, humans are 20 years ahead of it already. The Internet is exposing everyone for who they really are, and it's quite disgusting to me and should be to everyone else. I'll sum up what I mean by saying four words: FUCK YOU, HARVEY WEINSTEIN. This man is a VILLAIN in my industry, and I won't stand for people like him existing in this ecosystem any longer. These people that I'm going after have no idea what's coming for them, and they are some VERY powerful people. There's going to come a day in the next 18 to 24 months where I will gain their attention and I will look them directly in the eyes and tell them I've declared war on flushing out Hollywood. "Draining the swamp," if you will.

Now in order to take on this burden, I had to die that night. I had to shed everything, any and all materialistic things, and suffer through the worst experience of my life, because then I was able to build a suit of armor around me and now I fear nothing. When I tell people in my industry this, I tell them don't worry, I'll take all the arrows. Meaning I'll take all the spotlight and blame and shit-talking that will go on about me, and people will judge the fuck out of me. Good. Keep feeding me. Because people are dying. People are fucking hanging themselves in bathrooms and jumping off fucking *bridges*! How much more of a wake-up call does humanity need?! This industry has fucked everyone, and it's in desperate need for a cleanse, and I'm the one who's going to lead the charge.

So, I think that's about it. Now it's all out there—not like it isn't already—but now hopefully you have enough information for me to somewhat explain myself and my actions.

To go on record, I am following the request of a VOICE I heard, March 28, 2017, during a mental breakdown.

Oh, the podcast. Good news, I did it. I pulled it off. There was a lot of anxiety building up to March 28. I was on edge to say the least. What if I went crazy again? It's not, NOT possible, right? But nope, no mental breakdown. We had Bruce and Sandy over for dinner, played games, and then went to bed. No breakdown. However, I began throwing up violently at around 9 or 9:30 pm and continued to throw up every 10 minutes until about 7 am. I slept on the floor in the bathroom. At around 2 am, Abi became violently ill and starting throwing up every 10 minutes and did so until about 8 or 9 am. The next day, I sat on the couch, all day, in the exact same spot, doing the exact same thing I did a year ago on that same day, which was nothing. Strangely enough, Bruce and Sandy didn't get sick at all, despite eating the exact same thing we did. It was a casserole. Now, coincidence? Of course. Whatever negative energy out there that would like to see me not succeed in fulfilling my destiny? Yep. Sometimes I can feel it. That was it giving me a punch in the gut, reminding me it's still there. The darkness that I felt so many years earlier. It doesn't know who it's messing with now. I've transcended time and space and established a connection with everything the Universe has to offer, and I take that responsibility very seriously.

There's something in me that tells me I won't live to see 73. I think I died at 36 and will die again 36 years after that night. If I accomplish everything I have set in my mind to do, then that'll be just fine with me.

THE END

AFTERWORD

The reason I decided to include an afterword to this book is to give you all some context of how and when I wrote what you've just hopefully read. As you can tell by the cover of this book and/or from my Instagram feed, you'll see that I wrote this book in the spring of 2018. It is now early 2019, and I plan on publishing this book on the second anniversary of my breakdown, March 28, 2019. If I'm able to accomplish that, I will feel good about it. I didn't want to change too much about what I wrote because I want to keep the authenticity of where my head was at during that time. But a lot has changed since I wrote this book and what I am writing down now.

Abi and I are no longer together. We are together in the sense that she is and will always be my best friend, but she just couldn't do it anymore, and I don't blame her. Jesus, the shit's she's been through because of me—I could only imagine where her head has been over the last few years. There are still many things up in the air, but we are taking things one day at a time and, of course, making sure nothing affects Canon's life negatively because of our separation.

Abi is an empath. I am a narcissist. We could not be more opposite. She wants to give, and I want to take. We may be able to work incredibly well together but not romantically. I'm proud of us that we had the courage and the balls to recognize this now, instead of ignoring it and continuing to live in misery like so many other married couples do. There's a reason marriages fail so often. People aren't willing to be completely honest with themselves. They placate to the masses and will post all these apparently amazing times with their spouse and how great they are, etc., but when you actually pull back the curtain on their lives, both of them are fucking miserable. Because they are trying to live up to the guise that someone else has put in their heads, whether that be society, their parents, their friends, their siblings, whomever. I am here to tell you that you shouldn't give a fuck about anyone else or what anyone else thinks about *any* part of your life, especially your "partner."

Abi and I will still work together in the future, and like it's always been, people will be confused by that. "Won't it be weird working with your ex?" Of course. But not weird enough for me to not still want to. As hard as it is to deal with the physical feelings of going through our divorce, I'm strangely comforted by the fact that I knew this was going to happen. The VOICE told me I would have to be cut off from Abi. It was one of the feelings I had to go through in order to die that night. Just like I had to experience the feeling of separation from Daniel that night, I had to experience the feeling of separation from Abi. It was the thing I fought back most against that night. But I finally made the decision to accept it and now here we are, almost two years later, and I'm experiencing exactly what I was told would happen.

My opinion of my dad and his house has changed since originally writing this book. Much like I had to strip myself bare of everything in order to be able to build myself back up again, that house has strangely mirrored my own recovery. The house is still far from being done, but my God...the work that my dad has done on it thus far is exquisite. Whereas before I thought that house was dead and lifeless, all of a sudden I can see and feel its energy coming back, as I can with myself. There is no doubt that house will remain intact and in my family for generations to come.

I still see signs every day. The Raven has not gone away either. I've become nicer to Hauser and am sure his last few years will be a lot happier than his first nine or so years before.

On the one hand, I have nothing. I'm broke, I can't find a job, the tech-startup company I was working with all last year closed its doors, I've lost my wife, all of the clothes I wear were bought for me, I rely on my parents to give me money, I'm forced to take medication now that's supposed to make me feel "normal". I still have outbursts. And I still see my Demon and battle with it often.

On the other hand, I have never been more aware of who I am and what makes me happy in life than I have been now. I have a ridiculous amount of gasoline in my tank to begin attacking my mission. I have all the ammunition I need—I just have to crest over the hill so I can begin to deploy my battle plan. My son tells me on a nearly daily basis how wonderful of a dad he thinks I am, and my vlogs, posts, podcasts, etc., that I began doing all last year are starting to get some traction, and people are becoming inspired by them and my unabashed honesty and voice, and that's encouraging.

Do I still think I'll not live to 73? Who knows, but for the first time I think it might be a good thing to live as long as I can. A few months ago I went through probably one of the darkest times in my life and was contemplating suicide nearly every hour of every day. I would say, and I meant it: if Canon wasn't here, I'd have been gone a long time ago. People get uncomfortable when I talk about suicide so freely. I guess it's weird for them to hear about it, especially if it's someone close to me who cares about me, and maybe that's the problem. People aren't being honest with themselves anymore. They're living a false life and have a false sense of reality. The things people bitch about in their lives make me laugh. And then someone randomly kills themselves and people are confused by it. They give their "thoughts and prayers" but then go right back to not talking about difficult subjects.

Well, I only want to talk about difficult subjects, and instead of being afraid of someone else exposing me, I have chosen to expose myself before anyone else can. I refuse to give anyone else that power over me, of telling me what I can or should say and how or where I should say it. Fuck that. I will be as loud as I can be about the things that anger me: mental health, addiction, suicide, opioid and drug overdoses, people not being genuine, people "faking it" thinking they're happy because they got a new Louis Vuitton bag or some fresh new "kicks." I don't care about material things anymore. And I'm putting it down on paper to keep myself in check forever. Abi said something that is very true and very real. She said it a few weeks ago during one of our conversations about us being over. She said, "Ryan, you will never be able to achieve all of the things you want unless you find your own independence first." And she is 100% correct. I have never been completely independent in my life, ever. I've really almost never *not* lived paycheck to paycheck. I'm 38 years old, and I didn't buy a single birthday present for my son this past year because I couldn't afford to.

So I wanted to end with you all knowing that just because I've put pen to paper on everything that's happened to me, it doesn't mean things are all hunky-dory again. I struggle every single day as I'm sure so many of you do as well. I'm here to step out and scream from the top of my lungs that it's okay. Let me be your shield so that you all have the courage to step out and be honest with yourselves and to have the courage to share it with the rest of the world. I truly believe if we were all more honest with ourselves, the world would be a better place and there would be more peace instead of fighting.

I'll leave with this last thought…make no mistake, Hollywood, I'm coming after you. I'm not intimidated or afraid of your power, your wealth, your system. You disgust me in every way. You've been responsible for the deaths of so many amazingly talented people that your reign needs to come to an end. Every great empire falls at their height. The time is now. I know there are a lot of people who share in my beliefs but may be too afraid to stand up against it or do anything about it. Well, I am here to tell you that I will be the tip of the spear for us all to help change it. There is absolutely nothing you can say about me or try and use against me that I haven't already said about myself. People will get confused once I crest over that hill and begin to win all their statues and take all their money, but you will have no idea what I'm building right underneath your noses. If you didn't have your heads so deep inside the pockets of others, you'd be able to see *exactly* what I'm doing. But you don't, and you never will. And that is why this David will slay his Goliath. I'm on record now.

Come and get me.